Enjoy your garden
ROSES
IN COLOR

With an introduction by Claudia Binelli

DOUBLEDAY & COMPANY, INC.

Horticultural Consultants: Francis C. Stark, Professor and Chairman, Department of Horticulture, University of Maryland; Conrad B. Link, Professor of Horticulture, University of Maryland.

NOTE: The horticultural consultants have checked botanical terms against Bailey, *Standard Cyclopedia of Horticulture,* and other sources, but have used as the final authority Bailey and Bailey, *Hortus Second.* Some botanical varieties named by the authors have been retained even if they appear in none of our sources.

The original edition of this book was written in Italian, primarily for Italian gardeners. We have endeavored to preserve some of the rhetorical flavor of the Italian authors, while adapting the cultural and hardiness recommendations to the United States.

Picture credits. G. Tomsich, Rome: cover; Archivio B, Milan: 38, 40; Armstrong Nurseries, California (photos, C. Bryant): 28, 83; Conard-Pyle Co, Pennsylvania: 77; Fratelli Ingegnoli, Milan: 9, 25, 29, 47, 57, 73, 74, 89, 94, 105, 106, 108; Germain's Inc, California: 27; Michael Gibson: 5, 26, 102, 104; Gregory's Roses, Nottingham: 10-24, 30-37, 44-46, 50-56, 59, 62-70, 72, 75, 76, 78-80, 97, 98, 100, 101, 103; Kayebon Press Ltd, Cheshire: 7, 39, 41, 58, 81, 84-87, 90-92, 95, 96; G. Mazza, Milan: 1; S. Mc Gredy Roses, Portadown (photos, Kayebon Press): 42, 43, 48, 60, 61, 82, 88, 93, 99, 107; SEF, Turin: 2; G. Tomsich, Rome: 3, 4, 49, 71.
Drawings on page 12, 13 and 15 are reproduced from *Roses* by Peter Coats (Weidenfeld & Nicholson).

Translated from the Italian of Claudia Binelli

© Orbis Publishing Limited, London 1971
© Istituto Geografico De Agostini, Novara 1967

ISBN: 0-385-00899-6
Published under arrangement with
Ottenheimer Publishers, Inc.
Baltimore, Maryland
Manufactured in Italy by I.G.D.A.

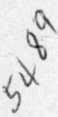
Table of Contents

3 Foreword

5 The rose in religion and symbolism

7 The principal wild roses

8 The cultivated roses

10 The largest and smallest rose

10 The rose-bush in the garden

11 Famous rose gardens and new varieties

11 How to grow roses

12 Insects and diseases

12 Pruning of roses

14 The rose in human life

14 The rose in art

15 The selection of garden roses

Another book on roses? Any rose-lover who sees a new publication in the store may be inclined to wonder how it can possibly be justified. At first glance, you might think there was nothing new to be said, no new problem to be studied, so fully have roses been dealt with by distinguished botanists and artists. But if you consider that about fifteen thousand species are being cultivated today, and two hundred new varieties are shown at international competitions every year, if you think of their commercial importance, of the thousands of acres on which they are grown all over the world, of their beauty both out of doors and in the house, it becomes clear that there is plenty more to be said about them.

This book deals first of all with the remarkable history of the rose from ancient times until our own day, and with what it has symbolized in the history of man. Country-lovers will find descriptions of wild species that anyone may find to admire, wild species that are the ancestors of many varieties of cultivated roses.

The origin of the cultivated rose is another fascinating subject. Imaginative growers have, down the years, managed to obtain a very wide range of color, and today, with all the scientific means at their disposal, and by the skillful crossing of roses, they are still patiently trying to produce a black or a blue rose.

Then, all down the centuries, both the flower and the fruit of the roses have had various uses, and today they are still used in the making of scents and cosmetics and medicinal products. They are commercially important as well, of course, as cut flowers, potted plants, and for display in the garden or in the house. Anyone wanting to grow roses in his garden or on a balcony in town will find advice on how to do so and on the diseases from which they may suffer.

The importance of the rose in art is also briefly discussed; painters and, even more so, engravers, have found it a constant source of inspiration.

There are many illustrations, with very full captions, which means that every part of the text is easy to follow and the best known species and varieties can be recognized.

The rose needs no introduction: its fresh, abundant petals, its superb color, its delicate scent and exquisite form all make it a truly regal flower. Every garden, however modest, needs to have roses in it. In fact, it is impossible to imagine the world without the rose, for it has been adorning the earth since time immemorial, cheering man from his earliest years and serving as a symbol of his history.

This book is dedicated to all who love roses, and who have found in them the wonderful harmony and beauty in which nature is steeped.

'The man with a rose in his hat', says a Mexican proverb, 'has the whole world' – because he has known the beauty of creation, and, in gazing at it, is happy.

Claudia Binelli

Rosa gallica

Published by Wm. Woodville, May 1, 1792.

The rose in religion and symbolism

From the earth's earliest days until the time of Christ, from the Middle Ages until our own day, the rose has been part of man's life on earth, and its origins are lost in legend and in mythology. All we know for certain is that it originated in central Asia, spreading eastwards to North America, and westwards to Asia Minor and Europe, but never crossing the equator.

In India they say the most beautiful woman in the world, the goddess Lakshmi, was born from a large rose, and in the East the rose was sacred to the goddess of fertility, whose priestesses wore wreaths of white roses on their heads. Confucius says there were rose gardens in ancient China and Japan, and a Chinese manuscript on roses is dated 500 BC.

The Incas in Peru, before the Spanish Conquest, grew them and called the rose-tree 'the bush of the sun'. When Christopher Columbus reached the West Indies he found roses there. But the real home of the rose in the ancient world was Persia: whole gardens were given over to it, superb rose-trees surrounded the city, the emperors themselves were skilled gardeners, and, in the luxurious Persian tradition, rich crowns were made of rose-petals stitched with raffia.

From Persia the rose was brought to Babylonia, where it was grown in the famous Hanging Gardens and became a symbol of the power of the state. There, Jewish exiles came to know and love it. But it came very much later into Egypt and Asia Minor, and flowers that are called roses in many ancient translations should in fact be called lilies.

The rose reached Greece in the fifth century BC, and Epicurus admired it. Homer never knew it, but Sappho called it, for the first time, 'the queen of flowers'. In Greek mythology it was said that Cybele created the rose because she was jealous of Aphrodite – and wished to create something more beautiful than the goddess of beauty herself. But when Aphrodite rushed to the wounded Adonis, tearing through a rose hedge and staining the flowers with her blood, the red rose was born. So the rose became the symbol of Aphrodite and of Aurora and Cupid, who accompanied her, representing love and its fleeting nature, and youth. It was also sacred to Harpocrates, the god of silence.

The Greeks were the first to use the expression that was later latinised to 'sub rosa', under the rose, to mean something secret and mysterious. This expression seems to have been used for the first time during preparations for the decisive battle of the Greeks against the Persians, which were made very secretly in a bower of roses, and although we cannot know for certain whether this story is true, we do know that the rose became a symbol of secrecy and that the term 'sub rosa' came down from ancient times into the Middle Ages, and spread all over Europe. Indeed, if a conversation were to take place in secret, a rose was hung on the ceiling, although, later on, this rose came to be made of plaster.

The Greeks considered it a flower for weddings, as well, and the women made crowns of roses, interwoven with branches of myrtle. But if it was worn on the brow or the breast, it was a sign of mourning.

From Greece the rose passed on to Rome, where it enjoyed a further period of splendor. In the early years of the Roman republic, roses were made into crowns which were worn by heroes and defenders of the state, and when the republic was in danger the wearing of roses was strictly forbidden. But later this changed, and under the Emperor Augustus roses were used in every type of decoration.

At feasts and banquets everyone, old and young, slaves, musicians and dancers, wore crowns of roses stitched with raffia; roses were twined around goblets, rose-petals dropped into the wine when toasts were drunk, and the cushions the guests sat on were filled with rose petals. Roses were used in the preparation of jellies, honey and wine, and rose petals were crystallised and eaten.

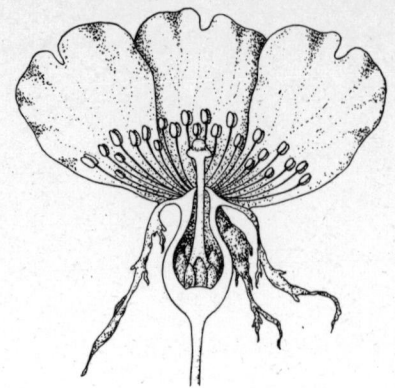

Line drawing of a wild rose flower: a simple flower, like that of the dog rose.

Section of a wild rose flower.

The rose-gardens of Paestum became famous, attracting large crowds when they were in flower, and were praised by Virgil and Ovid. The Romans also looked on the rose as a symbol of love and used it to decorate their graves. In April and May, during the feast of Flora, goddess of flowers, they held celebrations in honor of the rose, and often mentioned in their wills the kinds of roses they wanted on their graves, leaving bequests of money for their planting and upkeep.

Gradually, however, the Romans' pleasure in roses became luxuriant folly. The peasants cut down their orchards and olive groves to make space for them, elaborate hothouses were built to allow them to bloom in winter, and they were brought across from Egypt by sea. Unfortunately, we know nothing about the methods by which they were transported, methods which somehow allowed them to arrive in Rome still fresh. It would seem, indeed, that the Romans' extravagance over roses was something they learned from Egypt, where Cleopatra spent vast sums in order to surround herself with roses. Suetonius says that Nero spent the equivalent of about $120,000 on roses for a single banquet; so the Romans were clearly not far behind her in lavish expense.

With the coming of Christianity this extravagance came to an end; indeed, for a short time the rose was forbidden and forgotten. But soon it returned to favor and became the loveliest decoration of the churches on religious feasts. Once again it was used as a symbol of secrecy, and in 1500 Pope Hadrian had a rose carved on all confessionals, where for some time it had been the custom to hang a real rose that had been blessed.

There is some opinion that the prayer beads St. Dominic called 'rosaries' in 1208, which are still an object of devotion today, were first made from rose hips.

Legends grew up around the rose and many people used it symbolically. The Turks, for instance, say that the white rose originated from Mohammed's sweat and the red rose from his blood; so it is the sacred flower of the Mohammedans and until about 1750 it was the custom to wrap the babies of the Seraglio is rose-petals.

When the Roman empire in the west was overwhelmed by the barbarians, the Arabs carried on the traditions of the Persian and Babylonian gardeners and used roses extravagantly, like the ancient Romans. From about the year 1000, they managed to extract essences from roses, and to make rose-water through distillation; these scents were used to purify the mosques and other religious rooms. When North Africa and Spain were conquered the Arabs passed their love of roses on to their subject peoples.

Flowers were not considered important in the Middle Ages: people were too busy fighting and too many necessities were lacking for them to worry about the luxuries of life. But if the rose fell from favor as an ornament, it became important for its medicinal properties. Its fruit, rich in vitamin C, was an excellent remedy against scurvy, the most widespread of medieval diseases, and so it was grown in monasteries and spread all over Europe by the Benedictines.

It was only in France and England that the love of roses never died, in spite of wars and revolutions, and so it was in those two countries that the modern rose came into being. In France, at Fontenay-aux-roses, at Provins and in the marvellous gardens of Rouen, the Roman tradition had survived. In England a red rose, brought from France in the year 1200, was for centuries the symbol of the house of Lancaster, and a white rose symbolized the house of York. At the end of the 15th century, after the long and terrible Wars of the Roses, the two roses were united in the house of Tudor – and today the rose is still one of the symbols of the British royal house.

In Germany the rose had a very special symbolism. The bleeding wounds of warrior heroes were called rosebuds, the battlefield was known as a rose garden. Yet in the age of chivalry it was also connected with love, and love philters were distilled from roses.

After the medieval age Europe came to a scientific

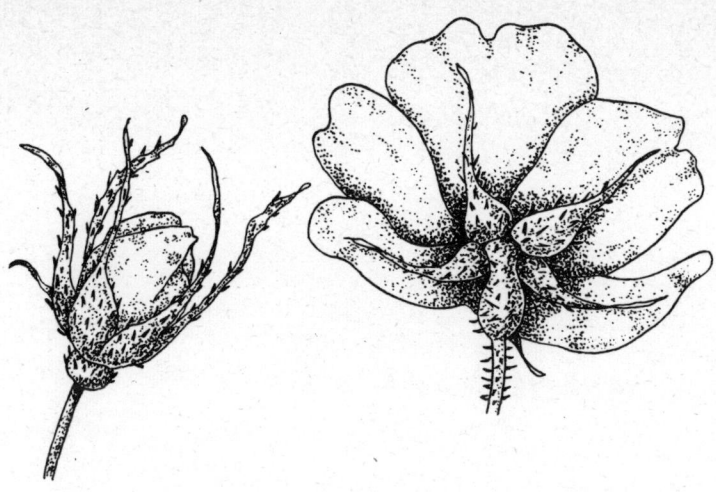

Bud with very long sepals; flower seen from below, of the *Rosa macrophylla*, showing the glandular hairs which cover the calyx.

period: printing was invented in Germany and botanists studied plants as they were, not as Aristotle had described them. Roses, grown according to the principles of Albert the Great and Pietro de' Crescenzi, were used in particular as hedges, and until about 1700, new flowers superseded them in many European gardens.

In 18th-century France Joséphine Beauharnais, Napoleon's wife, greatly encouraged their cultivation by creating the most famous rose garden of its time at Malmaison and commissioning the famous engraver Redouté to copy thousands of the flowers. After her death the garden was left to go wild, but the roses she had made famous continued to fascinate people and many rose gardens were planted by kings and emperors during the 19th century.

Feasts in honor of the rose were held and its cultivation was popular everywhere; the climbing varieties on walls, artificial ruins and Gothic gateways were particular favorites. People gave presents of vases shaped as pyramids or spheres, holding very neat and regular blooms all round them.

New varieties were already sold for fabulous sums during the last century and the enthusiasm for roses has continued until our own day, when it has given rise to a specialized industry.

Today, magazines on roses, and societies of rose lovers like the American Rose Society, teach people how to grow the flower and maintain its popularity. Cut roses are arranged in all kinds of ways: in bunches, in baskets, or with other flowers; from America the fashion has spread for displaying a single rose in a crystal vase. Roses are suitable for every occasion and today, as in the past, they are the very best flower for every kind of decoration.

A bouquet of long-stemmed roses always makes the most charming welcome for a distinguished visitor, and it is said that the then Aga Khan sent thirty thousand roses to Geneva when the League of Nations was launched. Even in the twentieth century heads of state may be welcomed by a shower of rose petals during an official visit.

Today the rose is as much of a symbol as ever, for its harmonious beauty still represents mystery, purity and love. So many associations have made this emblem of secrecy their own, like the anti-Nazi 'White Rose' group in recent years. Its regular appearance means that it is often used emblematically, for subjects that have nothing to do with botany.

And today, as in ancient times, a bunch of red roses means a declaration of love.

We now have splendid flower shops, where we can find roses in varied colors and with superb scents. But in spring and summer we can also still enjoy the beautiful wild roses in the woods.

The principal wild roses

In hedges and woods, in stony places, on hills and plains in many countries, we find the delightful wild rose; sometimes a species that has not been cultivated and has remained in its natural state. These are shrubs of the rose family and their stalks have strong curved thorns near their base.

Their leaves, which are a fine shiny green on the top side and paler on the underside, may be deciduous or evergreen, and have five to seven leaflets set on the axis of the leaf like the barbs of a feather. The flowers come out in May or June, singly or in pairs, on a single stem.

There are five green sepals surrounding five petals that are generally pink or occasionally white. Inside are a great many stamens, and the ovaries are in the swelling at the base of the flower.

The spurious fruit of the rose, called the hip, is generally red and in the shape of a fleshy bag, twisted at the top by the remains of the sepals and full of pips – the real fruit.

The most widespread of the wild roses is the dog-rose *Rosa canina*. It grows in hedges and woods to altitudes of 3000 feet above sea level, and flowers from May to July in most areas. Its petals are pink or whitish.

7

Buds and flower of the *Rosa involucrata:* note the completely bare stalk and calyx.

In the hedges and woods of Central Europe the *Rosa arvensis* is found; it has slender reddish-mauve branches, with white flowers that bloom in June and July.

Similar to the dog-rose is the *Rosa gallica*, which forms low bushes and has beautiful scented flowers, generally deep pink but sometimes bright or deep red.

On mountain slopes, around woods, grows the *Rosa cinnamomea*, a tall bush with large pink flowers that grow singly or in groups of twos and threes. The *Rosa pendulina* (synonymous with the *Rosa alpina*) grows higher up, and flowers from June to August; it has purplish or pink flowers and no thorns.

The flowers of the *Rosa moschata* and the *Rosa rubiginosa* have a very distinctive scent. The *Rosa moschata*, which has grown up naturally on the Mediterranean shores in particular, has white flowers in clusters and a musky scent; and the *Rosa rubiginosa*, which grows in stony, untended places, has resinous glands that give out a smell like russet apples.

In Italy, the *Rosa sempervirens*, which originated in the east, has become naturalized; it has white flowers, a strong scent, and blooms from May to July.

The moss rose *(Rose centifolia muscosa)*, is very beautiful and pure, and can easily be recognized because its stalks are covered with a great many small, soft prickles.

The prairie rose *(Rosa setigera)* is a native to the Central United States. *Rosa Virginiana; R. blanda* and *R. Carolina* are native in the eastern U.S. Some European species are found wild, having escaped cultivation including *R. multiflorea; R. canina* and *R. rugosa*.

Many other species are found in Europe, Asia and America. However modest they may seem, they are all important in the cultivation of roses, because they can be crossed with already hybrid roses and many of them are used in the propagating of the cultivated species.

Some of them make attractive garden shrubs in their own natural, unadulterated form, and they are still available for the domestic garden.

The cultivated roses

Through selection and hybridization, a great many types of roses have been created from the wild species. These vary in form, in color, in the richness of their petals and in their behavior. The roses that came to us from the east were probably the result of a great deal of selection already, and so different from their ancestors, the wild species.

Most experts believe that three species, the *Rosa centifolia muscosa*, the *Rosa gallica* and the *Rosa damascena*, came to us from south-east Asia, perhaps descended from a single common ancestor. The *centifolia* reached North Africa, Spain and the south of France and acclimatized itself perfectly, becoming the 'rose de Provence' or 'rose chou' or 'cent feuilles' of the French, and the *Rosa provincialis* of the Romans.

The ancient authors mention this rose, which later crossed the Bosphorus, passed into Germany and Holland, and was improved and widely grown.

In the next age the *Rosa gallica* came to Europe, possibly brought in by the Romans. It spread to northern France, especially to Provins, where in fact it was named the 'rose of Provins'. Its late-blooming flower had twelve generally red petals, it was cultivated all through the Middle Ages as a medicinal plant and was taken to England by the Duke of Lancaster, where it became part of the arms of the kings of England. The early settlers probably took it to America.

Another ancient rose is the rose of Damascus *(Rosa damascena)*, which has individual, drooping flowers with a charming perfume. It was brought by the Greeks to Marseilles, Carthage and Paestum, and became the Romans' rose. It was in fact in Italy, at Paestum, that it was seen to be 'reflowering', that is that it bloomed twice a year, and so the Romans called it *Rosa bifera* and the French the 'rose des quatre saisons'. It was destroyed by the eruption of Vesuvius and although the Arabs cultivated it and obtained rose-water from it, it reappeared in the west only about the year 1500.

8

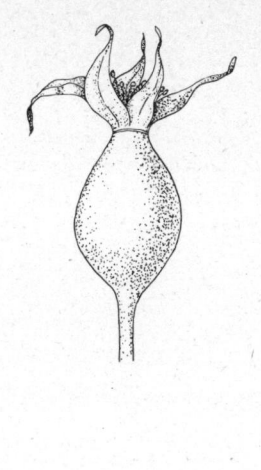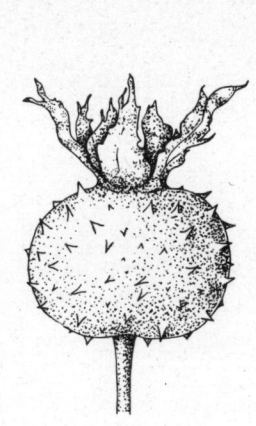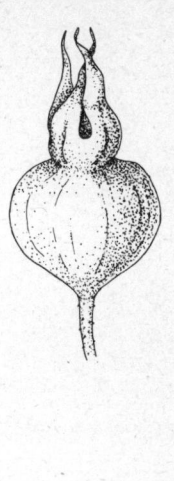

Left: Rose hip, shaped like an ampoule. Right: Spurious fruit: hip of the dog rose.

Left: Rose hip, globular, flattened top and bottom, with thorns. Right: Rose hip, globular and spiral.

The real revolution in rose growing took place at the end of the 18th century when the roses of Bengal and China reached Europe, in particular *Rosa indica* and the *Rosa sempervirens*. These and others were discovered in Canton by merchants of the East India Company, and reached England through Holland.

The *Rosa indica*, which already had many forms, had a scent like that of tea, and so the name tea-rose was given to its large, perfectly formed flowers, with their ten, or even fifteen, petals. Its leaves, which were long lasting and resistant to disease, were a dark shiny green. The *Rosa sempervirens* or Bengal rose, which bloomed for a very long period, had white flowers that grew in clusters.

When these and other species reached Europe, and the sexuality of plants was discovered (that is, about the end of the 18th century) rose-growers were able to do what they had only dreamed about before, and the richness of forms and colors we now know was achieved through hybridization.

Today, then, the old roses in our gardens have been joined by 'young' or 'modern' roses, less than a century old. The old roses include the original species gradually brought into Europe, and their hybrids; these are still known by their Latin names. The modern roses are generally hybrids and frequently it is impossible to trace their ancestry.

These new roses began to be grown in gardens in the 19th century as a result of the crossings made among the species that were already known. Then came the *Rosa bourboniana*, with its large, dark pink flowers, from the island of Réunion, and the *Rosa alba*, with its dazzlingly white petals and pleasant scent, from northern Europe. The many hybrids of all these species were called 'perpetuals', although in fact few roses really flower perpetually.

They were highly resistant to disease and achieved a wide range of colors, yet few of them have come down to us, because they were crossed with tea-roses, and formed new hybrids known as hybrid-teas which, though less healthy than their parent roses, had many petaled, delightfully shaped flowers and were very decorative. They became very popular in gardens, where they were especially suitable for making flowerbeds.

The end of the 19th century was important in the history of the rose, for in May, 1885, a French gardener named Pernet-Ducher happened to see, in the garden of the Tête d'Or at Lyons, a branch on a rose bush with flowers that were copper and yellow. This was a mutation, or what growers call a 'sport'; where, through some trick of nature, one branch on the bush 'sports' a different color.

These roses were a revelation to Monsieur Pernet-Ducher: in the gardens of his time there were no yellow or orange or two-toned roses.

From then onwards he spent his life seeking a yellow rose, and about forty years later, in 1920, he produced his masterpiece, 'Souvenir de Claudius Pernet', the yellow rose named after his son, who had been killed in the war.

This perfectly-formed rose, with its double flowers in a warm yellow, was the ancestor of all the reddish-orange roses and all the two-colored roses so fashionable today. The yellow varieties, though, perhaps because this ancestor of theirs was a delicate, greenhouse specimen, had little resistance and were short-lived. Most of them have disappeared from the catalogues but, through the use of stock with a stronger constitution, the modern yellow roses are hardy and reliable.

The climbing roses, derived from crossing *Rosa indica* and *Rosa moschata*, began to develop at the beginning of this century. Roses of this type in our gardens today are found on bushes that cling to supports and mostly bloom only once in summer. *Rosa multiflora* is used as a living fence for protection against animals and in particular, as anti-dazzle and crash barriers on the highways, with good effect. This is the species commonly used as the understock on budded plants.

The flowers of the climbing roses may be large, with

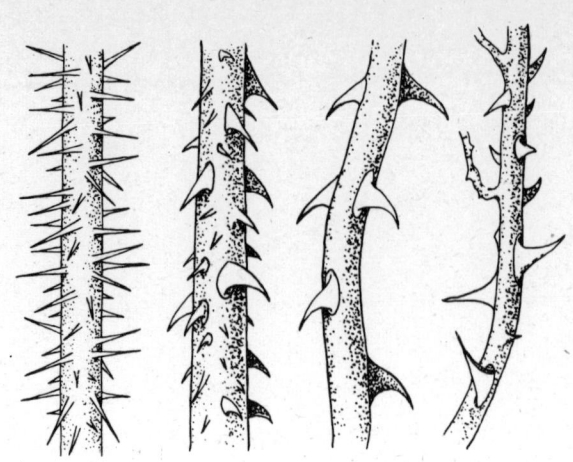

Various types of thorn on rose stems and branches: from left to right: needle-shaped thorns, beak-shaped thorns, crescent-shaped thorns pointing downwards, and beak-shaped thorns, some of which point upwards.

a great many petals, or simple, with only five petals, or half-double, with a double row of petals; but they all have the one characteristic, that they grow in clusters. Some varieties, among them Dortmund, Danse de Feu, and Aloha, are suitable for small gardens, while the splendid Mermaid seems more at home in a larger garden.

By being successfully crossed with tea roses, these climbing roses have produced some dwarf roses known as Polyantha Pompoms. They were the first miniature roses, and were also called fairy roses or Lilliputians; all of them are very small, with a large number of tiny flowers in clusters, and an extremely elegant air. They have no scent, but can be grown in pots very successfully.

Later these first dwarf roses were crossed with hybrid tea roses by the Danish grower Svend Poulsen, and produced the large, strong, Poulsen roses, that is, the Polyantha hybrid roses more recently known as Floribundas.

Today, these are very popular in gardens. Their flowers grow in clusters, are formed of five or ten fleshy petals, and are remarkably resistant to disease. Quite apart from their beauty, they are popular because they are easy to grow.

They are used a great deal to form flowerbeds in which what matters most is the general effect of the color, and they are particularly well liked by people who want the best results with the least amount of work. In recent years, though, they have been crossed again with hybrid tea roses, and their forms have become much richer. Tea roses have also been improved: they are delicate but much prized, and are always shown in the most important international competitions.

The largest and the smallest rose

Whenever we look at nature we like to know which is

the largest and which the smallest of each species, and it is always hard to say, when creation has so many forms. With roses, if we consider the fifteen thousand kinds that exist today, it is nearly impossible.

If by 'largest' we mean the number of petals in a rose, then certainly the Baccara rose wins: it has a maximum of seventy-two petals in flowers that are two to three inches in diameter. But the flower may have few petals, ten to fifteen for instance, yet have a record diameter of four inches, like the red Anna Wheatcroft or the coral-pink Ascot.

Some roses, the red, scented Tally Ho, for example, or the yellow Burnaby, have flowers with a diameter of about four inches and a large number of petals as well. An effect of size is also achieved by a rose like the Ama, which has large double flowers in compact clusters and fine orange leaves.

Similarly, it is hard to choose the smallest rose: among miniature roses, the Baby Masquerade, with flowers only one inch in diameter, may be considered the smallest, and among non-dwarf roses, the smallest are roses like the Cocktail or Border Coral, which have flowers less than two inches in diameter.

The rose-bush in the garden

From early summer to late fall the rose bush is the finest ornament of any garden, particularly suited to forming straight-sided or circular flowerbeds with roses of the floribunda type, that is, with medium-sized bushes bearing flowers in clusters that bloom regularly and constantly.

They should be planted about twelve to fifteen inches apart. Rose bushes of a single color should be grown in each bed, with a few small rose trees to break the monotony.

These rose trees are very useful as hedges or protective borders, and so are tall rose bushes, but the distance between them must be at least a yard if they are used in this way.

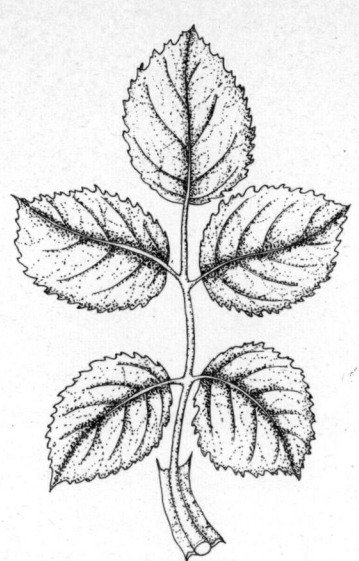

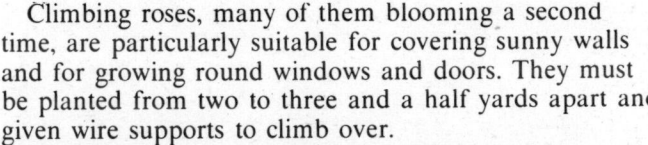

Schematic drawing of a spray of rose leaves, consisting of five small oval serrated leaves; the stalk has no thorns.

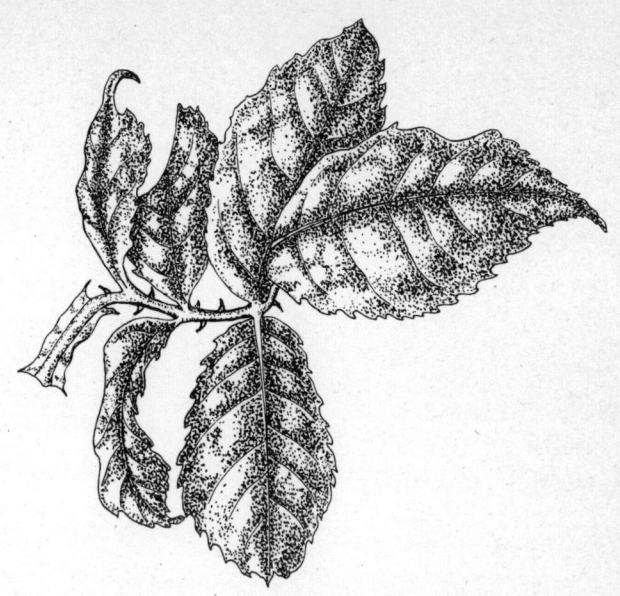

Leaf of *Rosa indica*, var. *ruga*: a hybrid between *Rosa chinensis* and *Rosa arvensis*. The stalk is prickly; as in other roses, there may be an even number of leaves because one of those in the end pair is missing.

Climbing roses, many of them blooming a second time, are particularly suitable for covering sunny walls and for growing round windows and doors. They must be planted from two to three and a half yards apart and given wire supports to climb over.

If pillars are to be covered, or trellises of roses formed, rambler roses are needed with small flowers that do not bloom twice but have a rich growth. A bed of roses for cut flowers is also useful in the garden, and for this hybrid tea roses with long stalks are the most suitable.

Rose-growing in pots needs expert advice; miniature roses, hybrid tea or floribundas, which can be grown in a small amount of soil, are all suitable.

Famous rose gardens and new varieties

Roses are shown to best advantage in a rose garden, that is, a sunny garden where nothing else is grown. The beds have regular geometrical shapes and are at least a yard apart; lawns show up the color of the flowers and small rose trees, pergolas, pilasters and climbing roses provide variety and interest.

In specialized gardens, cultivators experiment, crossing species and seeking continuously, with infinite patience, for new colors such as black and delphinium blue; here they prepare the new varieties which are shown at competitions, held in the world's most famous rose centers.

Rose growers are faced with great difficulties. Each cross between two roses produces an enormous number of seeds, and the same crossing often has to be repeated thousands of times. At the Meilland gardens in Antibes, for instance, forty-five thousand seeds are grown each year, and through selection, within five or six years, only three or four remain which may be released as new cultivars.

Every year about two hundred new roses are

produced all over the world. They must conform to certain standards of behavior and size, and must be tried out for at least three years at the rose center where the competition is held. The winner generally receives a large prize and is hailed as an inventor; and his variety is protected and patented.

Some excellent public rose gardens are found at the Brooklyn Botanic Gardens, Brooklyn, N.Y.; Hershey Rose Garden, Hershey, Pa.; Missouri Botanical Garden, St. Louis, Mo.; and Golden Gate Park in San Francisco, Calif. In Europe there is a famous rose garden in Geneva, and the Bagatelle park in Paris, where the 'rose of the year' is chosen is well known too. In France there is also the rose garden at Lyons, where modern roses were born, and where a competition limited to French varieties is held, and the rose garden of Haÿ-les-roses, which includes a rose museum.

The most beautiful rose garden in the world is said to be that of the Oeste Park in Madrid, started from scratch in 1954. In England, there is Queen Mary's famous rose garden at Regents Park in London, and Winston Churchill's rose garden, the Golden Walk at Chartwell, planted in 1958 to celebrate his golden wedding.

In Italy, a competition is held in the rose garden in Rome, planted in 1928 on the ruins of the Domus Aurea and enlarged in 1948. Another famous rose garden is in Turin; this is part of the Valentino gardens, and was planted in 1961 to celebrate the centenary of the unification of the Kingdom of Italy.

How to grow roses

As a rule, the rose has an important quality – through its wide distribution it is adaptable, and that is why it can be found in many gardens. First, however, select a site that receives sun for the major portion of the day. Avoid locations near large trees or shrubs.

Roses will grow in any soil from a sandy loam to heavy clay, provided it is well drained. In preparing the

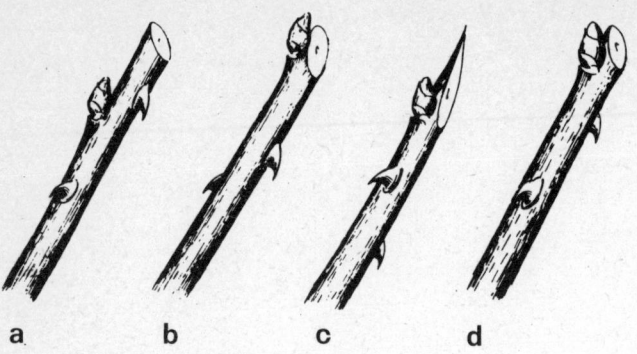

a b c d

Some of the wrong ways **(a, b, c)** and the right way **(d)** of pruning. Facing page (top): a rose bush before pruning, with tangled branches and weak growth; the same bush thinned out; and a hybrid tea pruned to within 6 inches of the ground, with the buds left pointing outwards to make a shapely bush. The diagrams (facing, below) show how grafting is carried out. **1:** The bud is just visible in the axil of the leaf. **2–3:** A sliver of bark is removed with the bud and the axil. **4–5:** The wood from the inside of the bark is removed, and the piece trimmed neatly at each end. **6–8:** A neat T cut is made in the bark of the stock, the bud is slipped in, and tied tightly in place with raffia so that all air is excluded. New growth soon follows.

soil for planting, add organic matter such as peat moss, composted organic matter such as leaves and garden refuse or rotted manures. Use liberal quantities – a two to three inch layer over the surface is added and thoroughly spaded into the upper 6 to 8 inches. A preferred practice, especially in previously uncultivated areas or in heavier soils, is to dig a trench 12 to 15 inches wide and 15 to 18 inches deep and incorporate the organic matter into this soil. Well prepared soil is essential to a successful rose garden.

A soil test should be made before preparation starts and corrections or additions of nutrients made. A soil acidity level of ph. 5.5 to 7.0 is preferred for roses. If it is more acid, lime should be added, the amount based on the soil test. Superphosphate is used to supply the potassium.

Bare rooted plants should be planted as soon as they are received. This is done in late fall or early spring. Container grown roses may be planted in any season.

Established roses should be fertilized with a complete fertilizer, such as 5–10–5, in early spring and immediately after the first blooms are finished. If they are watered as needed, then a third application is made in early fall.

During the summer, water the plants as necessary, and cultivate to eliminate weeds. To reduce summer maintenance, use a summer mulch for weed control, as well as to conserve water.

Insects and diseases

There are several insects that can cause damage to the rose. An infestation of aphids may descend on the young growths at an early stage and at the same time, or a little later, caterpillars may be detected on the leaves. Usually, with the latter, they are few and may be picked off and destroyed. Pesticides are available to control both.

Sudden changes in temperature will bring an attack of mildew at any time. Once noticed, this can be controlled by spraying. Continue this throughout the season at 10 to 14 day intervals.

More serious are the fungus diseases, which, if ignored, may result in partial or complete loss of foliage. The most serious is black spot which does not generally appear much before August. However, the rose lover may prevent this by using a proprietary fungicide spray every ten days from the beginning of May. It is best to consult a reliable supplier for his advice as to the most suitable fungicide, and use according to instructions.

Pruning of roses

Pruning is necessary to encourage healthy growth, which, in turn, promotes good blooms. It also maintains a shapely bush but it must be expertly done. Arguments have raged and will continue to do so, as to the best time to commence. Generally speaking, the end of February is a good starting point, according to the season – all pruning must be suspended during frosty weather – and bearing in mind that the further north one goes, so it becomes progressively later.

Hybrid Teas A start should be made with the hybrid teas; first remove all weak growth and shorten the remainder to 8 to 12 inches from the soil, according to strength, always cutting to an outward facing bud. Vigorous cultivars should be more lightly pruned. Newly planted bushes should be cut 6 to 8 inches above the soil, to encourage root action and robust growth.

Floribundas Here, the stems should be cut to 15 to 18 inches long. The older wood may be removed if there are several younger stems. New bushes should have all growth reduced 8 to 12 inches.

Ramblers Prune in summer after flowering. If there is sufficient new growth – five to seven canes, then remove all old wood. Where the previous year's growth has to be retained, cut back approximately ½ of its length. Newly planted ramblers should be cut back to 12 to 18 inches.

Climbers Remove all weak growth. Retain the young

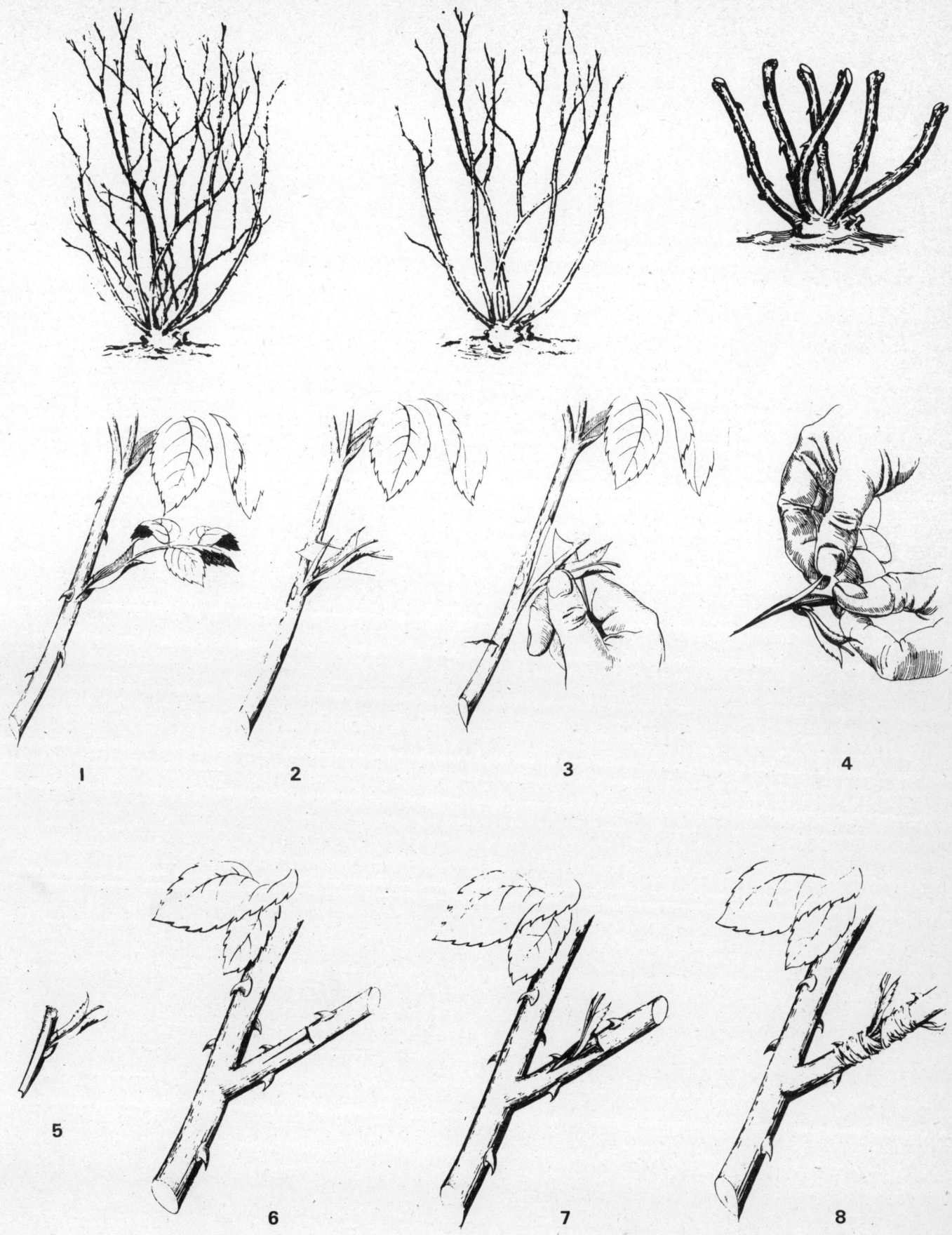

1   2   3   4

5   6   7   8

growth and older wood where necessary. Do not prune or cut back for one year after planting.

Standards "Tree Forms" Prune as for hybrid teas and floribundas. Keep a sharp watch for growth from stem of the stock and remove immediately.

Weeping Standards These are rambler roses budded at the top of five to six foot stems, the strong growths reaching to the ground. Most effective where umbrella wire trainers are used. Prune as for ramblers, tipping the young growth.

Rose species No pruning required, except to remove dead or very weak wood.

Old-fashioned roses After the first year, cut out dead or weak wood and crossed branches. It may be essential at times to remove some branches altogether, when the plant is extremely bushy.

Pruning in the fall This is not really pruning at all, but the reduction of all strong growth by approximately half to prevent wind-rocking. This is done after all leaves have dropped. This is a cause of many fatalities among roses during the winter months.

Removal of suckers Suckers are those growths coming from the stock below where the bud was inserted, distinguishable by their different appearance or number of leaflets – seven. It is customary to cut these off at ground level, but this only encourages more growth, to the detriment of the host. The soil should be carefully moved and the shoot traced to its base. Hold firmly, tug sharply and it should become detached from the root. Replace soil immediately and firm well.

The rose in human life

In ancient times and in the Middle Ages love philters were made from roses; but quite apart from this magical use, roses were used as excellent deodorants, in times when washing was unfashionable.

In ancient Rome, roses were used in the preparation of jellies, honey, wine and desserts, and today the fruit of the dog rose is used to make preserves and jam. In the east, their petals are used in the making of sweets and to flavor liqueurs and ice-creams.

The important medicinal qualities of roses were already known in Roman times, and in the Middle Ages all apothecaries used them because their fruit was rich in what we now know as vitamin C.

Today rose water has a pharmaceutical use in the cure of eye diseases; the petals of the *Rosa centifolia* are used in laxatives for children, and those of the *Rosa gallica* provide astringent liquids and are used in rose hip syrup.

Rose water and essences made from roses are most useful of all in the perfume industry, which came to us from the east – from Arabia and Persia in particular. Rose water is extracted from the *Rosa moschata* and the *Rosa damascena*, by rapid distillation with steam or a solvent, and this is used to purify and improve the skin; distilled again, it becomes an essence used in perfumes.

The perfume industry is important in Nice and Cannes, and even more so in Eastern Europe and the near east – in Bulgaria and Turkey mainly; but recently the production of artificial essences has reduced the production from rose flowers.

The rose in this century is important as a decoration, and thousands of people, including rose experts, are employed in producing cut flowers, potted bushes and garden plants. The greenhouses in the Netherlands are especially successful in the production of cut roses. In the United States they are an important part of the florist industry with the greenhouse production especially developed in the northern states, in Colorado and in California.

The rose in art

In a few lines it is impossible to deal adequately with the broad subject of the rose in art. Every form of art, poetry, painting, sculpture, interior decoration, has been influenced by the rose and continues to be so.

Since ancient times poets have praised the rose and

used it as a symbol of youth, of the beloved, of the fleetingness of earthly things and of vanity. This began with Sappho, continued through Virgil, the *Roman de la Rose*, Poliziano and Lorenzo the Magnificent, and still survives today.

Other artists have found the rose a subject worthy of contemplation and love. It is engraved on ancient coins and painted in the frescoes of Pompeii; we find it in Flemish and Renaissance paintings, on Gothic gates or musical instruments.

The best way of ending a book on roses is to mention once again the French engraver Redouté, whose copies of the roses in the Empress Josephine's garden at Malmaison are unsurpassed.

The selection of garden roses

The following is a selection of cultivars (varieties) to select from for planting in the garden, separated into the major classes and grouped by color. Each year nurserymen introduce new cultivars and drop some of those that have proved to be less satisfactory. These new cultivars are from breeders from all parts of the world. Many of these have been especially evaluated in the All American Rose Trial Gardens throughout the United States and may be designated as an All American Selection for that year. Only a select few receive this distinction. For the gardener who wishes the newest – try these selections. However, many of the cultivars in these lists have been on the market for many years, which proves their general usefulness and satisfaction as a garden plant.

The classes of roses are:

Hybrid Tea – large flowers, occasionally stems with more than one bloom.

Grandiflora – medium to large flowers, two to three flowers per cluster.

Floribunda – medium sized flowers, clusters typically flat topped.

Polyantha – small flowers, clusters typically large, pyramidal or cone shaped.

Miniature – small flowers, dwarf plant.

Hybrid Perpetual – large flowers, generally only one period of spring bloom.

Climbers-Ramblers – long stems, suitable for use on a trellis or support. Ramblers typically produce many shoots with flowers in clusters. Climbers have fewer stems, large flowers singly or in small clusters. There are climbing forms of many cultivars.

Shrub Roses – these are the species or hybrids of larger growing kinds, grown primarily for their use as flowering shrubs. This class generally includes the so called "old fashioned" roses.

15

R. centifolia muscosa (**4**) is the original form of the Moss Rose, which was enormously popular in Victorian times. Its buds and flower stalks are covered in numerous little pointed glands which are sticky and scented and resemble moss if you do not look too closely. R. centifolia muscosa was a sport from one of the older *centifolia* roses and is pink, but there are also white, deep red and pink and white striped forms.

The first three pictures on this page show typical examples of wild or species roses of the kind from which all our garden roses are descended. They are single, with five petals and attractive stamens, and most, though not all, produce colorful red or orange hips in the fall. *Rosa canina* (**1**) appears in the ancestry of the Alba roses, one of which is the White Rose of York, and another of which is the Jacobite Rose of Bonnie Prince Charlie. It is still common today in most parts of the world, growing in hedgerows and wild places, its long, thorny canes clambering up through other bushes and into low trees. Its delicate flowers appear only for a comparatively short time in early June, and in common with all species roses there is no repeat blooming. It is probably not a garden rose itself unless you have plenty of space, as there are other species which are much more showy. *R. pendula* (also called *R. alpina*, **2**) is very similar, but is found growing at greater altitudes. *Rosa spinosissima altaica*, **3**, is a sub-species belonging to the big *spinosissima* family, which will grow in the poorest, sandy soil. Many of the hybrids are first-rate garden roses and some small enough for the rockery. Others go to the opposite extreme: for example, Frühlingsgold is a huge and magnificent shrub which will reach 8 ft in height, with long arching canes spreading out to about the same distance and which bear along their whole length, in early June and July, pale, creamy yellow semi-double flowers of extreme beauty. They have a sweet, delicate scent. Frühlingmorgen is another, but not quite so big, and it does have some further blooms in the fall.

5

5 Pascali Hybrid Tea. Lens, 1963. Queen Elizabeth × White Butterfly. The only white Hybrid Tea to stand rain well and be reasonably free from disease. It has medium-sized, high-centered flowers, which sometimes have a touch of cream in their coloring. Strong and upright to 3 ft. Glossy, dark green leaves. Good for cutting.

6

7

8 9

10

6 Queen Elizabeth Floribunda (UK) or Grandiflora (USA). Lammerts, 1954. Charlotte Armstrong × Floradora. One of the tallest of roses and not really suitable for bedding, as it can grow up to 6 ft or so, though fairly hard pruning can keep it below this. The foliage is dark and handsome, semi-glossy and generally healthy. The flowers are of a soft, light pink. Sometimes they come in medium-sized clusters and sometimes singly, but always on long stalks, which makes them suitable for cutting. Only slight fragrance. For the back of the border or for a hedge.

7 Iceberg Floribunda. Kordes, 1958. Robin Hood × Virgo. (Also known as Schneewittchen and Fée des Neiges). The white blooms, shaped like those of a camellia, are carried all over the bush and not just at the top as in so many Floribundas. They come in medium-sized trusses on the rather slender branches, and the bush is rarely out of flower. It may reach 6 ft unless pruned. Some mildew and some black spot are possible, but rarely bad. One of the very best roses, which will stand up to prolonged rain very well.

8 Percy Thrower Hybrid Tea. Lens, 1964. La Jolla × Karl Herbst. Large, fragrant, rose-pink, well-formed double flowers on a vigorously growing bush that is, however, inclined to sprawl. This means that in wet weather the blooms tend to droop, and pruning the canes to an inward-facing eye is needed to keep the plant more compact. The foliage is dark green and glossy.

9 Royal Highness Hybrid Tea. Swim and Weeks, 1962. Virgo × Peace. Also known as Königliche Hoheit. A very upright grower which will reach 5 ft and not spread out very much. It is a profuse bloomer, with beautifully shaped, high-centered flowers of such a soft light pink that they give the impression of being white from a distance. They are not very good in wet weather, but when cut hold their perfect form for a very long time. For this reason it is a favorite rose with exhibitors on both sides of the Atlantic. Very dark green, leathery foliage, which is reasonably healthy.

10 Invitation Hybrid Tea. Swim and Weeks, 1961. Charlotte Armstrong × Signora. Long, pointed buds develop into $4\frac{1}{2}$ in, double, high-centered flowers of a rich salmon-pink, merging into yellow at the petal bases. A compact and bushy grower, free blooming, and with good, glossy foliage. Strongly scented.

11 Mischief Hybrid Tea. McGredy, 1961. Peace ×
Spartan. This is one of the best bedding roses. It is healthy,
vigorous but not too tall, and almost continually in flower.
The blooms can be up to 4 ins across, but when they come in
clusters, as they tend to do especially in the autumn, they are
likely to be rather smaller. However, they are almost always
well-shaped with a good high center, and at their best and
biggest can be used for showing. They are fragrant and of a
strong, salmon-pink, and grow on a strong, upright bush of
about 2 ft 6 ins or a little more. The light green foliage is
generally healthy. This rose is the winner of a number of top
national awards, and fully deserving of them.

12 Jenny Fair Hybrid Tea. De Ruiter, 1967. Tropicana ×
unknown. Rather globular pink flowers which are well
scented. They grow on a rather slender and upright bush and
are well set off by the dark foliage, which may need watching
for mildew. Free blooming, but not really bushy enough to
make it the best of bedding roses.

13 Dr. Albert Schweitzer Hybrid Tea. Delbert-Chabert,
1961. Chic Parisien × Michèle Meilland. Large, 5–6 in
flowers of 30 to 35 petals, and of a light cerise-pink with a
paler reverse. They are well formed on opening but can
become rather loose after a short time. A very vigorous,
upright bush with dark, glossy foliage, which is very good for
bedding and gives an especially impressive display in the
fall, though it may be affected by both mildew and black
spot. The flowers are fragrant.

14

15

14 City of Leeds Floribunda. McGredy, 1966. Evelyn Fison × (Spartan × Red Favourite). This is a comparatively new rose and as such it is unwise to be too dogmatic about its qualities. It can take a number of years for a rose to settle down and show its true form (see Tropicana), but certainly City of Leeds does look like a winner and it is a first-rate floribunda, Evelyn Fison (Irish Wonder in the USA) as one of its parents. The rich salmon flowers are carried on good-sized trusses, and come very freely with a quick repeat, but they can spot after prolonged rain. The plant is of upright growth with dark green foliage, which is generally quite healthy. Little or no scent.

15 Love Token Floribunda. Gregory, 1964. Parentage not known, which means it is probably a chance seedling, for which the bees were responsible. A good rose for all weather as it is practically rain-proof. The trusses of peach-pink flowers are well-spaced; the flowers themselves are of medium size and double, though they have little scent. Growth is vigorous and spreading and the leaves large, dark and glossy. When young they have an attractive purplish tinge. Not particularly prone to any of the usual rose diseases.

16 Tip Top Floribunda. Tantau, 1963. Parentage not known, but this particular German breeder quite often does not give particulars of his breeding lines. This rose should not be confused with the miniature rose known as Tip-Top, and in fact, registration of its name was rejected because it was found that the miniature was still in commerce. However, despite all this, it is a good rose with well-formed, double, salmon-pink, scented blooms which grow in very large clusters and very freely. The growth is strong and bushy, on the low side, which makes it very suitable for small beds, though it can make a spectacular display in a large one. Medium-green leaves.

17 Vilia Floribunda. Robinson, 1960. Parentage unknown. Large clusters of single, coral-pink flowers, very freely borne. They are scented, though not strongly, and come on a moderately vigorous bush with dark green, glossy foliage. It is a good bloomer in the fall.

18 Tropicana (Super Star in the UK). Hybrid Tea. Tantau, 1960. (Seedling × Peace) × (Seedling × Alpine Glow). This is a rose that took the gardening world by storm. for its light vermilion blooms were of a color never before seen in roses and have, in addition, an almost luminous quality which makes them stand out against all others. A number of roses have been bred from it since then, and have almost captured its unique coloring, but not quite, and certainly none of them can equal Tropicana's four Gold Medals and numerous other awards. The flowers may come singly (in which case they will be large, up to 5 ins at their best and of the high-pointed form that makes them good for showing) or in clusters, particularly in the autumn. They last for a long time in water and have a sweet scent. They are produced very freely on an extremely vigorous bush, which is likely to grow to about 3 ft 6 ins or 4 ft, with dark, glossy, leathery foliage. All this on the credit side, but Tropicana is not a rose that has worn well, at least in some areas. It appeared for a number of years to be extremely healthy – with its other qualities, to be nearly perfect, in fact – but then, for no apparent reason, it started to get mildew badly, and this is a continuing trait; however it does not occur everywhere it is grown, so that the rose is worth taking a chance with. There is a climbing version, or sport, on the market as well.

17

18

19 Dearest Floribunda. Dickson, 1960. (Seedling × Spartan). This rose does not like rain, which is unusual in a Floribunda – though surprisingly it does well in the fall, when the air tends to be damp. But apart from this one fault, it has everything to recommend it and has long been a favorite. The clusters of very large and very double flowers, freely borne, are of the most enchanting rosy salmon shade, and scented. They grow on a strong, upright bush to about 2 ft 6 ins, on which the foliage is dark and glossy and not particularly prone to disease. During a long hot summer you will get an almost non-stop display, and it will carry on flowering into the late months of the year, even until the first frost.

20 Tombola Floribunda. De Ruiter, 1967. Amor × (Ena Harkness × Peace). The truss has large, well-shaped flowers in the half-open stage but they do not keep their good form when open. However, this does not matter too much as the overall effect of the truss is a fine blend of salmon-orange with a touch of light carmine and gold at the bases of the petals of each flower. The bush is strong-growing, rather upright, and the leaves are a good, glossy green. Not, unfortunately, very quick to repeat.

21 Elizabeth of Glamis (Irish Beauty) Floribunda. McGredy, 1964. Spartan × Highlight. Her Royal Highness, the Queen Mother, gave her permission for this rose to be named after her. Presumably because some people outside the British Isles may not know who Elizabeth of Glamis is (or that Glamis is pronounced *Glarms*) the name was changed to Irish Beauty for the USA. Under any name it is one of the loveliest roses, with medium-sized clusters of large (4 in) double flowers in a beautiful soft salmon color, somewhat deeper in the autumn. It has won top awards both as a rose itself, and separately for its fragrance, which is quite an achievement for a Floribunda. The plant is vigorous and bushy, with very free bloom and a quick repeat, carrying on until the frosts. There are, however, one or two possible drawbacks. In some districts its health is suspect, and some growers say that it does not transplant well. In fact there are nurseries which do not stock it for this reason; but certainly it does move quite happily from the nursery to the garden in most cases, and it may simply be that some types of soil do not suit it. It certainly gives little trouble on light, sandy soil, and all in all is a rose worth taking a chance with.

22 Fragrant Cloud (Duftwolke) Hybrid Tea. Also known as Nuage Parfumé. Tantau, 1963. Seedling × Prima Ballerina. This rose is considered by many to be the best Hybrid Tea produced since Peace. The large, full blooms are produced in incredible profusion, and tend to come in clusters. These should be at least partially disbudded to obtain the maximum size. Their shape is always good, with a high, firm center in the early stages. Strong fragrance; the color is a vivid geranium lake, which dulls a little with age. The leaves are large, glossy and dark green. Generally it is very healthy and stands wet weather well.

23 Pink Parfait Floribunda-Hybrid Tea type, or Grandiflora. Swim, 1960. First Love × Pinocchio. A very good rose in one of the quieter colorings that are so useful when one wishes to separate the stronger-colored roses in a bedding scheme. The flowers are of medium to light pink, yellow at the base of the petals, and with an apricot reverse. They are quite large and of a good shape, though they eventually open flat. There is a slight fragrance, and the 2 ft 6 in to 3 ft bush is well branched and very free-flowering with, as a rule, medium-sized trusses. The leaves are mid-green and glossy. A good all-weather rose and also quite healthy.

24 My Girl (Curiosa) Floribunda. De Ruiter, 1964. Dacapo × Seedling. Large clusters of very double, cupped, deep salmon blooms distinguish this rose, in which the weight of the trusses may weigh down the rather slender canes and cause the plant to sprawl. It is a vigorous grower nonetheless, and has dark green, coppery foliage which may suffer from black spot.

25 Blue Moon (Also Mainzer Fastnacht or Sisi) Hybrid Tea. Tantau, 1964. Unknown seedling × Sterling Silver. A large, well-shaped double bloom of mauve – lavender color, which is very fragrant. The bush is robust and upright, usually reaching 3 ft high, and it has large, deep green leaves which are generally healthy but will need watching for black spot in a bad year. However, it does tend to be of rather uneven growth and not to send up many new strong growths from the base of the plant.

26

26 Ernest H. Morse Hybrid Tea. Kordes, 1964. Parentage unknown. Ernest H. Morse has established itself as a strongly fragrant, bright, turkey-red rose of good form and size, which can produce exhibition quality blooms but is equally good for garden display. It seems to flower almost without ceasing, and although its many blooms lose their first bright glow rather quickly, they are still attractive. Growth is very robust, upright but bushing out well, and probably reaching 3 ft. Very good, large, semi-glossy dark green foliage, which rarely suffers from disease. It does not mind rain.

27 Chrysler Imperial Hybrid Tea. Lammerts, 1952. Charlotte Armstrong × Mirandy. One of the best red roses ever raised and, despite the fact that it is over twenty years old, still worth growing. The blooms are large, high-centered, and keep their shape well. They are crimson-red with darker shadings, but have one drawback that is common to so many roses of this color; they blue with age and become much less attractive. Regular dead-heading would, of course, get rid of this problem. One other characteristic that Chrysler Imperial has in common with most other reds is that it has a strong, sweet, fragrance. Growth is robust and upright to about 3 ft, and the large leaves are a matt, dark green. They should be watched for mildew. A number of good, dark red roses have been bred from this variety, including one of the best modern ones, Mister Lincoln.

28 First Love Hybrid Tea. Swim, 1952. Charlotte Armstrong × Show Girl. Yet another American rose bred from the prolific Charlotte Armstrong. This one has medium-sized blooms of 25 to 30 petals, which are pale pink with deeper shadings, and which last particularly well if cut for the house. They are fragrant and grow on a bushy plant, that spreads out well and will reach 3 ft. Mid-green, semi-glossy foliage. A good rose for bedding.

29 Manitou Hybrid Tea. Swim, 1957. Parentage unknown. A rose that would be more popular if it were more prolific with its blooms, for when they do come they are very large and very lovely, opening cupped and with plenty of petals, resembling deep coppery pink peonies. However, it is rare to get more than four or five on the plant at any one time, and there is a fairly long gap between the first and second flushes. The bush is vigorous and spreading and has deep green semi-glossy foliage. Not noticeably scented, but stands rain well.

30 Coral Queen Elizabeth Floribunda or Grandiflora. Gregory, 1966. Queen Elizabeth × unknown. There is clearly some doubt about the origin of this rose. Its official pedigree indicates that it comes from Queen Elizabeth, crossed with something else, as does Scarlet Queen Elizabeth, but in habit it looks like a sport on the line of White and Yellow Queen Elizabeth. Certainly it has its known parent's vigor and is a tall, robust grower, free-flowering, the blooms coming singly and in clusters. They are of a deep, coral pink, double and about 3 ins across, opening cupped. They are also fragrant.

27

28   29

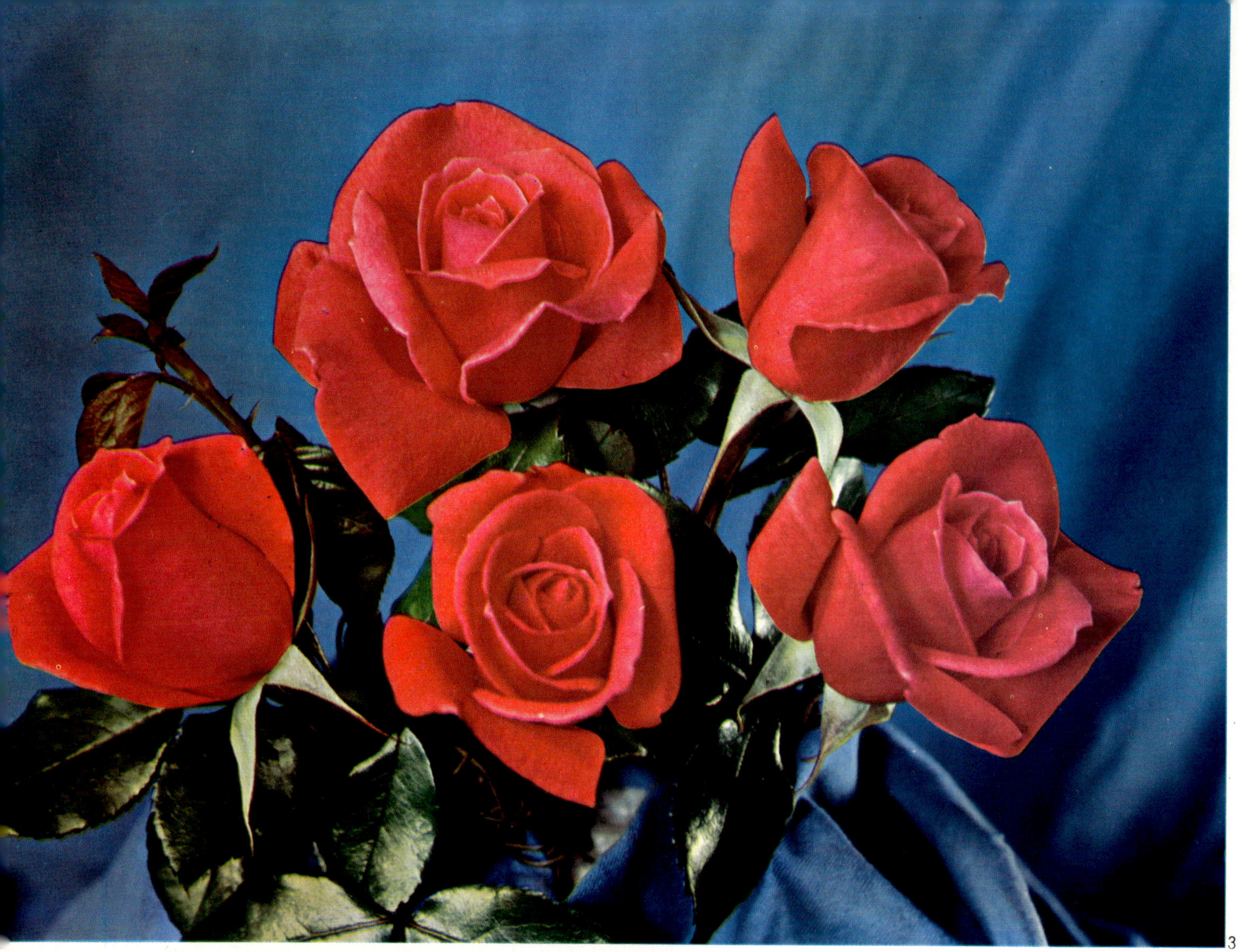

31

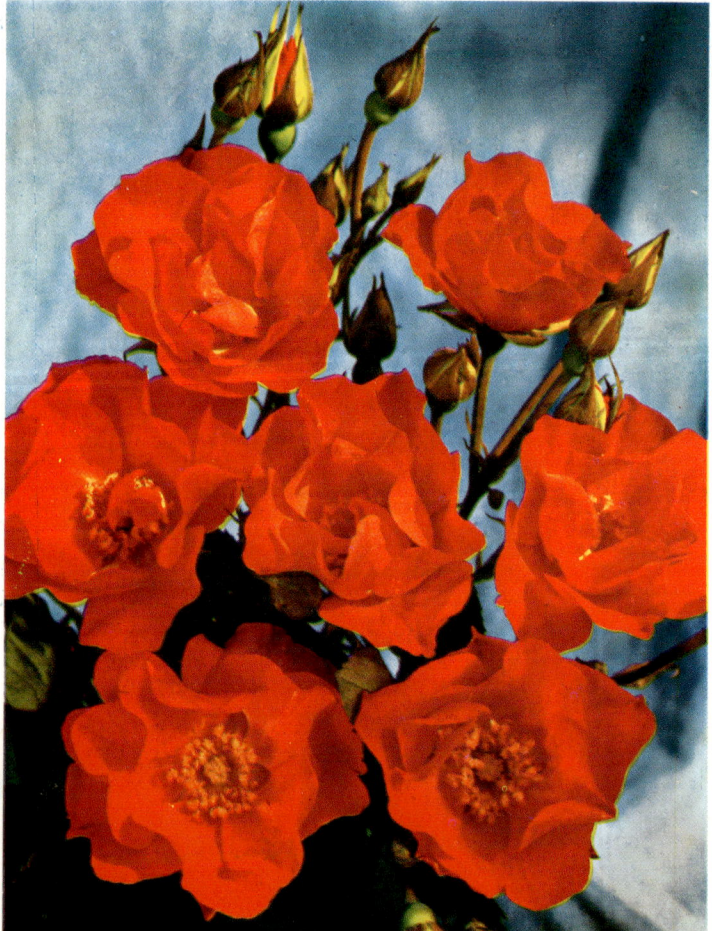

31 Coralita Climber. Zombory, 1964. (New Dawn × Geranium Red) × Fashion. A short climber, or it can be grown as a shrub, for it will not go much over 6 ft. The dark red buds open to large, very double orange-coral flowers, which are borne extremely freely. Good, dark, leathery leaves. A useful rose for a pillar.

32

33

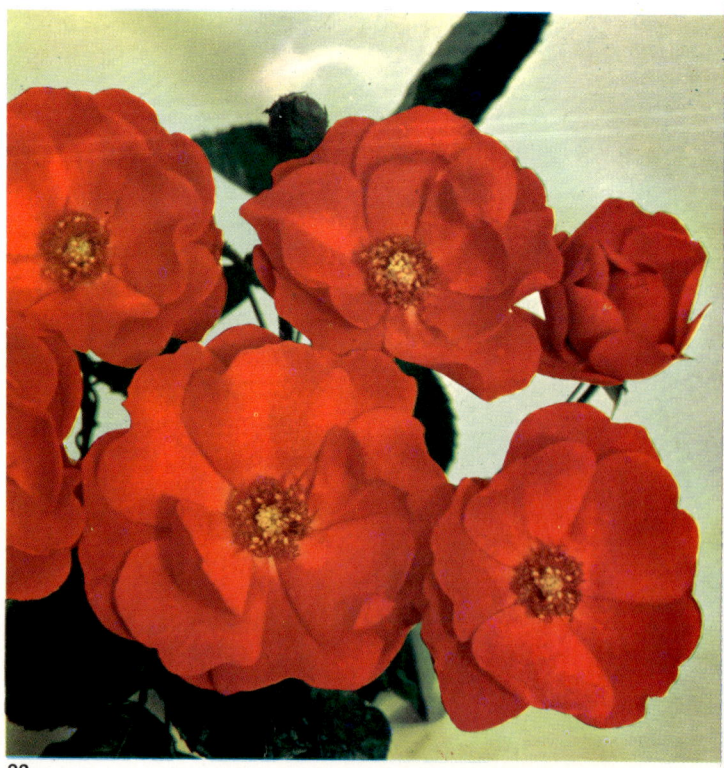

34

32 Maria Floribunda. Gregory, 1965. Unknown seedling × Border Beauty. The flowers of this rose are large for a Floribunda, being something like 3 ins across, and semi-double. They form large trusses, on which the flowers are well-spaced, only slightly fragrant, and of a very bright orange-scarlet. The strong-growing upright plant has dark, glossy leaves. Very free with its blooms, this was one of a number of good, if not outstanding, Floribundas in the scarlet shades that did not quite reach the top of the sales charts.

33 Paprika Floribunda. Tantau, 1958. Märchenland × Red Favorite. Paprika was one of the early ones of the same group as Maria, and it did make the grade, due not only to the fact that the competition at that time was not quite so fierce, but also because it was simply a very good rose. The flowers are even larger than those of Maria, semi-double, turkey-red and borne in enormous trusses. Growth is strong and the plant branches out well. It has plenty of glossy, olive green leaves; good in all weathers.

34 Wendy Cussons Hybrid Tea. Gregory, 1963. Independence × Eden Rose. Three Gold medals for this one, and it deserves them all, for it is very nearly the perfect garden rose and one that is equally good for exhibition. It is scarcely ever out of flower and carries masses of large, perfectly formed, high-centered blooms which seem to be impervious to rain. These are of a bright cerise-pink, and are also marvellously fragrant and will keep on coming until well into the fall. The plant is on the tall side, but it branches out well and has glossy, dark green leaves with a hint of red about them. It is not quite proof against mildew, but generally healthy.

35

36

35 Strawberry Fair Floribunda. Gregory, 1966. Orangeade × unknown seedling. Very vigorous and bushy with dark green foliage which sets off well the trusses of scarlet, double flowers. These are of medium size (about 2 ins) and are slightly fragrant. Very free bloom and quite a good repeat.

36 Evelyn Fison (Irish Wonder) McGredy, 1961. Moulin Rouge × Korona. Yet another of the vast number of scarlet and orange-scarlet Floribundas. This one, however, has been outstanding, mainly because the bright scarlet, 2 in flowers seem to be virtually indestructible.
Quite unfading in even the strongest sunshine, their short, tough petals enable them to stand up equally well to heavy and prolonged rain. They come in trusses which are usually medium-sized, though several times a year the bush is likely to send up truly enormous ones; the size of these, combined with the lasting power of the flowers when cut, make this a favorite rose in the Floribunda classes at shows. They have only slight fragrance. The bush is compact and spreads out well, growing to about 2 ft 6 ins, with mid- to light green very glossy leaves, which are normally very healthy. Evelyn Fison will flower well into the fall and has a good repeat.

37 Lancastrian Hybrid Tea. Gregory, 1965. Ena Harkness × seedling. A very fragrant, crimson-scarlet and well-shaped rose, growing on a strong, upright bush. The leaves are light green and glossy, with sometimes a tint of crimson. This rose is a good one which seems to have been rather over-shadowed by others of the same coloring which were introduced at about the same time. It is particularly good in the fall, but a tendency to mildew is a disadvantage.

38 Baccara Hybrid Tea. Meilland, 1956. Happiness × Independence. A rose that has more petals than almost any other, ranging in total between 72 and 82. They are, however, quite short, so that the globular bud opens well and the flowers as they develop are first cup-shaped and finally flat. As they last extremely well in water and have good long stems, this rose has for long been grown very extensively under glass for the cut flower trade. If you buy bright geranium-red roses at a florist, as likely as not you will be getting Baccara. In fact it is probably a better rose for this purpose than for the garden, at least in a damp climate. It was bred in the heat of the south of France. It is a strong and upright grower to about 3 ft, which is on the tall side for bedding in in modern small gardens. The foliage is dark and leathery.

39 Champs-Elysées Hybrid Tea. Meilland, 1957. Monique × Happiness. A good bedding rose that has been around some time, and has probably not been grown as widely as its qualities deserve. It will make a first-rate, colorful display, its large, cupped, crimson-red double flowers, coming in great profusion and repeating well and quickly, though they are only slightly fragrant. It forms a strong, upright bush to 2 ft 6 ins or 3 ft with good foliage.

39

40 Christian Dior Hybrid Tea. Meilland, 1961. (Sondermeldung × Happiness) × (Peace × Happiness). At its best a good rose for exhibitors, for the blooms come mainly one to a stem and are large, full, and high-centered. The inside of the petals is a beautiful velvety scarlet, with a rather duller scarlet on the reverse, but there is only slight fragrance. Growth is strong and upright, rarely exceeding 2 ft 6 ins. Will want watching for mildew and black spot.

40

41

42

41 Lilli Marlene Floribunda. Kordes, 1959. (Our Princess × Rudolph Timm) × Ama. Large, semi-double, crimson-scarlet flowers on large trusses, with however, only slight scent. The strong, well-branched plant, which will grow to 2 ft 6 ins, has mat, medium- to dark green foliage which often has bronze tints; the stems are plum-colored when young. Good in the rain but may suffer from mildew. This rose should not be confused with Marlene, another Floribunda from the same breeder. The latter has noticeably smaller leaves and smaller flowers of a brighter red, and is much shorter in growth. It is an excellent dwarf rose for small beds or for edging larger ones.

42 Finale (Also Ami des Jardins). Floribunda, Kordes, 1964. A low-growing compact rose, useful for the small bed and small garden. The flowers, which come in good-sized clusters, are quite large, double, and of an attractive salmon-rose. Little scent but good weather resistance. Light green, generally healthy foliage.

43 Uncle Walter Hybrid Tea. McGredy, 1963. Detroiter × Heidelberg. No doubt because of one of its parents, Heidelberg, which is classified as a Floribunda-Shrub, is a very tall-growing rose which is often used in the shrub border itself. It is too tall and probably too ungainly in growth for bedding. It will reach at least 5 ft, but the canes, though naturally upright, can be weighed down by the weight of bloom, which comes very freely. Probably it is best to put it at the back of the border or among other shrub roses so that it has something to lean on, and where its rather untidy habit of growth is concealed. The blooms are lovely, large, double, crimson-scarlet, and of a good, high-centered form, though they are only slightly fragrant. The foliage, which can be sparse lower down, is of a good, glossy dark green and leathery in texture. It is not proof against mildew.

44 Orange Sensation Floribunda. De Ruiter, 1960. Parentage unknown. One of the best and gayest bedding roses so far produced, particularly so in its color range; it is orange, shading to light vermilion at the petal edges. The latter color intensifies as the flower ages. The blooming is extremely prolific and the flowers come on large trusses, of which there seem to be an endless succession. The flowers themselves are medium-sized, with a pointed center at first and then opening slightly cupped and sweetly fragrant. Prolonged rain can stain the petal edges a rather unattractive red, but generally this rose stands up to bad weather as well as most, and showers will not affect it. Its habit of growth is very vigorous, spreading wide, so that it may be advisable to plant the bushes farther apart than usual, say at 2 ft intervals. It will rarely exceed 2 ft 6 ins in height. The leaves are mat, medium green and very plentiful, but are not proof against black spot and mildew, at least on light soils; the mildew particularly attacks the stalks of the flowers unless spraying is carried out. On better soils this tendency is not so apparent, but in any case it is a rose that is well worth a little extra trouble.

43

44

45 Orangeade Floribunda. McGredy, 1959.
Orange Sweetheart × Independence. Large, 3 in.
semi-double flowers of a glowing bright vermilion-
orange, which take on a deeper tone and lose a
little of their brilliance with age. They open quite
flat and have only slight fragrance. The well-
spaced trusses are of varying sizes but some can be
enormous, and they are very good for exhibiting as
they last well when cut, like most Floribundas. The
growth is very robust with good, strong canes,
upright but well branched out so that the flowers do
not come just at the top of the plant. The leaves are
very dark green and semi-glossy but, as with the
majority of orange roses, they are likely to need
spraying against black spot. This is because they
are all reasonably closely descended from a species
of Persian rose which was particularly prone to the
disease and which has handed the tendency on to
its offspring and their descendants. Nevertheless,
Orangeade is a very good rose indeed, repeating
well and fast, and will make a spectacular bed. A
climbing sport is also available.

45

46

46 Spanish Orange Floribunda. Gregory, 1966. Parentage unknown. Not a very well-known or widely grown rose, though there would still seem to be time for it to catch the public's fancy, as it is comparatively new. It is surprising how long it can sometimes take for a good rose to make its mark. That first-rate Hybrid Tea, Prima Ballerina, for instance, was introduced in 1958 and is only now beginning to be widely grown. In this case it was a question of sheer merit, plus the fact that it is one of the most strongly scented of modern roses, that gradually gained Prima Ballerina its recognition; but Spanish Orange may not be a rose of quite such outstanding quality. As its name implies, it comes in the orange range of colors with freely blooming trusses of small (1½ ins) very double flowers, which do rather resemble oranges. They have some fragrance and appear on a strong-growing but not very large bush, with dark, glossy leaves.

47 Beauté Hybrid Tea. Mallerin, 1954. Mme. Joseph Perraud × unnamed seedling. The flowers of this rose do not have a great many petals, which tends to make them open quickly. They are, however, of a lovely blend of orange-yellow and apricot and are beautiful in all their stages, from the long, tapering buds to the fully open blooms, which last a long time on the plant and are quite proof against rain. Only slight fragrance, but great profusion of bloom, which will carry on well into the fall. The leaves make a good frame-work for the flowers, being dark green and semi-glossy. Black spot should be watched for. The plant is quite vigorous, branches out well, though it can be rather spindly. Up to 2 ft 6 ins in height.

48 Chinatown Floribunda, though sometimes classed as a shrub rose. Poulsen, 1963. Columbine × Clare Grammerstorf. This is one that will certainly go up to 4 ft if not 5 ft, but it bushes out well and can make a handsome specimen shrub. Its strong canes need no support and are clothed almost down to the ground with large, attractive, glossy, light green leaves, which are usually proof against disease. Normally it will bear many trusses of up to seven or eight 4 in, very double yellow flowers, the color intensifying toward the center of the bloom and with sometimes a touch of pink on the petal edges. The second flowering is not as profuse as the first and there will not be a great many blooms in between. From this point of view it behaves more like a Hybrid Tea than a Floribunda.

49 Raymón Bach Hybrid Tea. Dot, 1938. Luis Brinas × Condesa de Sástago. A Spanish rose that is not seen much nowadays and which has large and very double (probably 80 petals), rather globular, blooms. They are strongly fragrant and of a bright orange, which pales a little towards the petal edges. A robust grower with glossy, dark green foliage.

52

53

50 Vienna Charm Also known as Wiener Charme. Hybrid Tea. Kordes, 1963. It has not been possible so far to breed a robust and healthy rose in a deep, coppery orange, but as this color happens at the moment to be a great favorite with the rose-growing public, breeders keep trying. It was thought at first that the German breeder, Kordes, had succeeded when he produced Vienna Charm, which has the most magnificent, high-centered, fragrant flowers, good enough for showing when at their best. But the plant on which they grow once more turned out a disappointment. It is vigorous enough, but tends to be rather uneven in habit, with the likelihood that it will send up single, enormously long shoots, well above the rest. This makes it look untidy and so not really very suitable for bedding, where uniformity of growth is usually wanted. However, this fault would not be too serious for such an attractive rose if it were not for the tendency of the canes to die back in any but the very mildest of winters, often right to the base, so that one loses them all together. In fact it is not uncommon for the plant to be killed.

51 Cover Girl Hybrid Tea. Von Abrams, 1960. Sutter's Gold × (Mme. Henri Guillot × Seedling). The long, pointed buds open into 5 in, double, high-centered flowers. They are in blends of light orange, copper and gold and slightly scented, and come in great profusion on an upright, bushy plant with glossy, dark green leaves.

52 Dr. A. J. Verhage Hybrid Tea. Verbeek, 1960. Tawny Gold × Baccara seedling. A most attractive golden yellow rose, the color deepening towards the centers of the medium-sized double flowers. The edges of the petals are pleasingly scalloped, which gives them a 'different' look, and they are scented. This rose is generally considered to be best under glass and it is widely used in the cut flower trade as its blooms, apart from generally coming singly to a stem and being produced very freely, last a long time when cut. But it will do very well in the garden, where it forms a smallish but reasonably vigorous bush with small, dark green, glossy leaves that seem to be very healthy.

53 Amarillo Hybrid Tea. Von Abrams, 1961. Buccaneer × Lowell Thomas. Exceptionally fragrant for a yellow rose, this one has large, high-centered blooms of rich gold on strong flower stems. It is vigorous, upright, and free of bloom, reaching 2 ft 6 ins to 3 ft. The leaves are leathery and light green. Not too quick with its repeat flowering.

54 Golden Treasure Floribunda. Tantau, 1965. Parentage unknown. Deep yellow double blooms on good trusses make this a colorful, cheerful rose, though the yellow does fade after a time as with most Floribundas of this color. The flowers are fairly large, up to 2½ ins, shapely in the early stages, and have a slight scent. Tall, strong growth and glossy, dark green leaves.

55 Buccaneer Unusual, in that it is known as a Hybrid Tea in Europe, but as a Grandiflora in America, which just goes to show how confusing the classification of roses can be. Swim, 1952. Golden Rapture × (Max Krause × Capt. Thomas). Buccaneer belongs to the group of very tall yellow roses, which includes Golden Giant and Gold Crown, all of which are too lanky to grow other than at the back of a border. Buccaneer is more prolific with its blooms than the others. They are of medium size, buttercup yellow, and cupped in shape when fully open. They have only a slight fragrance. The growth is vigorous and upright, probably to at least 4 ft, and the leaves are mat and green.

56 Arthur Bell Floribunda. McGredy 1965. Clare Grammerstorf × Piccadilly. One of the better yellow Floribundas, though no-one has produced a perfect one yet. All, with the exception of Allgold, which tends to be irregular in growth, fade to creamy yellow in strong sunlight, and Arthur Bell is certainly not proof against this failing. However, its large, full flowers, golden yellow at first, are still attractive when they turn to cream, and have the advantage that they are extremely fragrant. Good, mid-green foliage on an upright grower above the average in height, probably going up to 3 ft.

57 King's Ransom Hybrid Tea. Morey, 1961. Golden Masterpiece × Lydia. Undoubtedly the best pure yellow Hybrid Tea for general garden use as it is much more compact in growth than most and is unlikely to top 3 ft. The flowers are not over-large, but are of a good shape, with the outer petals reflexing nicely. They are borne freely with a quick repeat, though they are only slightly scented. The dark green, plentiful foliage may suffer from mildew.

58 Mary Poppins Hybrid Tea. Lens, 1965. Belle Etoile × (Michele Meilland × Tawny Gold). Also known as Lady Sunshine and not to be confused with another Hybrid Tea called Mary Poppins, which is shell-pink and was raised in the USA by Morey in 1967. One of the few yellow roses with a true rose perfume. Of medium height, it would be good for bedding if it had more flowers at any one time. When they do come, they are very large and of a good form. Mid-green leaves which may get black spot.

59 Golden Jewel   Also known as Bijou d'Or and
Goldjuwel. Floribunda. Tantau, 1959. Goldilocks ×
Masquerade seedling. There is little doubt that this would
be one of the best yellow Floribundas of all if only it were
more continuously in flower or even if, after a rest in the
middle of the summer, its second flush of bloom were better.
In its first flowering it is magnificent, with trusses of up to ten
very double, bright yellow, fragrant flowers like 3 in
pompons. They last on the bush a very long time and the
individual flowers stand up to rain well. However, they are
rather close together, and if one that is fading should get wet
the petals can be prevented from falling cleanly and can
spoil the buds forming underneath. It is as well to shake them
out. The foliage is dark and glossy and very healthy. The
bush will grow vigorously to about 2 ft 6 ins, branching well.

60 Norris Pratt   There seems to be some doubt as to
whether this is classed as a Hybrid Tea or a Floribunda.
Buisman, 1967. Mrs. Pierre S. du Pont × Marcelle Gret.
Both these parent roses are Hybrid Teas, which should make
it a Hybrid Tea as well, but its United Kingdom introducer
describes it as a Floribunda, perhaps because its tendency is
to flower in clusters with great profusion. The deep yellow,
unfading blooms are of classic Hybrid Tea shape, large, and
grow on a bush of moderate vigor. Leaves dark and leathery.

61   Bossa Nova   Hybrid Tea. McGredy, 1964. Leverkusen × Buccaneer. Big, 4 in, double blooms in a strong golden yellow that seems to be quite unfading. Large, glossy foliage on a vigorous plant which is rather above average height. Healthy, but not over-generous with its flowers between the two main flushes, though it is reasonably free during them. Watch for black spot.

62   Baby Masquerade   Miniature. Also known as Baby Carnaval. Tantau, 1956. Tom Thumb × Masquerade. While this is a true miniature rose, one of its parents is the Floribunda Masquerade, and it is very like it in many ways on a small scale. It is one of the tallest of the miniatures and will make a very bushy plant (which is likely to need a lot of thinning out at pruning time) reaching as much as 15 ins in height, while the average for miniatures is about 9 ins. The flowers come in trusses as on the parent variety, opening from ovoid buds; they are chrome yellow at first, passing through pink to rose red, all colors being on the truss at one time as the blooms open in succession. Coming very early into flower, Baby Masquerade almost always has some bloom showing, right through into the fall and will make a good edging for a bed of larger roses. Because of its size it is less likely to be swamped by them as some of the other, smaller, miniatures may be. And, flowering early, it will give some color before the other full-sized roses are out. It needs to be watched for mildew.

63   Simple Simon   Miniature. de Vink, 1955. (*Rosa multiflora nana* × Mrs Pierre S. du Pont) × Tom Thumb. This is one of the smaller of the miniatures, not over 6 ins tall, but it is one of the best, giving little trouble. During its long flowering period it is covered in clusters of tiny blooms of carmine-rose, which have a yellow tinge at the petal bases. The flowers are double and the foliage glossy.

64   Coralin (Carolin, Carolyn or Karolyn).   Miniature. Dot, 1955. Méphisto × Perla de Alcanada. Coral pink blooms, large, and of Hybrid Tea shape. They grow very freely on a low, bushy and compact plant which will reach 8 ins. One of the most attractive of the miniatures.

44

63

64

Miniature roses, of which a selection is shown on the preceding page, these two pages, and the two that follow, are miniatures in the full sense. They are not just rose bushes with small flowers, but the size of the plant, the leaves and the flowers are all in perfect scale. It is possible nowadays to obtain miniature standard or tree roses, and miniature climbers as well. They all have the same requirements as their larger cousins, and also some of the same weaknesses; they, too, can get mildew and black spot and be attacked by aphis. But they have the charm of anything that is tiny and neat. Pruning will probably have to be done with nail scissors and consists of cutting out over-crowded growth and any dead wood, and the tipping back of the other shoots.

65 Yellow Doll Miniature. Moore, 1962. Golden Glow × Zee. Quite a tall one, which will reach 12 ins. The pointed buds open to fine, Hybrid Tea-shaped flowers, very double and with 50 to 60 petals, fragrant, and of a good, deep yellow. The leaves are dark green and glossy. Though tall, it is also bushy.

66 Little Flirt Miniature. Moore, 1961. *Rosa wichuraiana* × Floradora. A cross between a species rambler and a Floribunda, it is difficult to see how this ended up a miniature, but it did – and a good one too. The blooms are fragrant, bright orange-red, and with a yellow reverse to the petals, giving a very gay effect. Masses of bloom on a bushy plant that will reach 9 to 10 ins, and which has light green leaves.

65

66

67

67 Baby Darling Miniature. Moore, 1964. Little Darling × Magic Wand. Small, double flowers of about 20 petals of an orange-pink. Dwarf, bushy growth to about 10 ins. A descendant of the Gold Medal winner, Little Darling, and inheriting many of its good qualities.

68 June Time Miniature. Moore, 1963. (*Rosa wichuraiana* × Floradora) × (Etoile Luisante seedling × Red Ripples). Half the parentage is the same as Little Flirt, but the result is very different. The small, many-petalled flowers are light pink with a deeper reverse. They grow in clusters on a bushy, compact, 10 in plant, which has glossy, mid-green leaves.

69 New Penny Miniature. Moore, 1962. (*Rosa wichuraiana* × Floradora) × unnamed seedling. Once again some of the same parents have produced a different result. The flowers are only semi-double, small, scented and of a strong orange-pink. Plenty of them on a good bushy grower with shiny leaves, that will reach 9 to 10 in.

70 Eleanor Miniature. Moore, 1960. (*Rosa wichuraiana* × Floradora) × (Seedling × Zee). Very small and very double flowers, opening from slim, pointed buds to a coral-pink which deepens as the flower ages. A good, free bloomer that will go up to 12 ins and has leathery, glossy leaves.

68

Miniature roses are often sold in pots and the implication is that they are good house-plants. This is only partially true, as they will not do well if they are kept in the house all the time, especially in the dry atmosphere of central heating. For the best results they should be kept out of doors until they are just coming into bloom and, when the flowers are over, taken outside again until the next flowering. They are perfectly hardy and can safely be left out of doors all winter, though in extreme climates they will need winter protection, like other roses. The pots should be plunged in the soil and watered if they dry out. The best way to grow miniature roses is in a rockery garden (provided that they have a deep, cool root run), in stone troughs on a terrace, or as edgings to a bed of larger roses. It is also possible to make a complete miniature rose garden with them, which will need either extremely fine grass or paving between the beds. Ordinary grass can overwhelm the small plants.

69

70

71 Fire King Floribunda. Meilland, 1958. Moulin Rouge × Fashion. Full, very double fiery scarlet blooms in large trusses. The flowers eventually open flat and are scented, and are carried on the plant until well into the fall. The leaves are dark green and the rose is a very strong-growing one, upright but bushy. This rose was a worthy All-American Winner in 1960, and originated in France.

72 Circus Floribunda. Swim, 1956. Fandango × Pinocchio. Also an All-American Winner, with several Gold Medals to its name as well, this is a rose that has been popular everywhere – and deservedly so. It is one of the best of all Floribundas and gives a tremendous show of flowers over a very long period, repeating remarkably quickly. The blooms are probably up to 3 ins across, very double, and are carried on large trusses, opening cupped. They are scented (though not very strongly) and open bright yellow, shaded with pink and salmon. Gradually the colors merge to a delicate apricot-orange. They are just about rain-proof and will open in the dullest weather. The healthy, bushy plant will reach 2 ft 6 ins.

73 Modern Times Hybrid Tea. Verbeek, 1956. A sport from Red Better Times. A great many of the old shrub roses are striped pink and white, particularly among the *gallicas*. As these figure largely in the parentage of modern roses it is rather surprising that there are not more Hybrid Teas or Floribundas in this very attractive combination. Those that are striped (not invariably in pink and white) have all been sports, so one of their ancestors is probably making its presence felt. Modern Times is such a rose, red, striped pale pink to white, and fragrant. It has profuse bloom which grows on a robust plant with light green foliage, which may get mildew. Unfortunately the colors, though bright and contrasting well when the flower first opens, tend to fade somewhat rapidly, so that the overall effect is very soon that of a pale pink rose.

74 Bajazzo Hybrid Tea. Kordes, 1961. Parentage unknown. A strong-growing Hybrid Tea with large, well-shaped and very fragrant blooms of a velvety texture, deep red and with a white reverse to the petals. An upright plant with mid-green foliage, it could be more free with its blooms in between the two main flushes.

71

72

73

74

75 Charleston Floribunda. Meilland, 1963. Masquerade × (Radar × Caprice). If you live in an area where black spot and mildew are prevalent, do not read any further, because Charleston is particularly prone to both. In other respects it can be recommended as a very vigorous grower to about 3 ft, with dark green, glossy foliage and very showy blooms. They are large, on good-sized trusses, and of a startlingly bright yellow, flushed crimson. Unlike its parent, Masquerade, the colors do not change or merge into each other, and in every respect except that of health it is a more attractive rose.

76   77

76 Doreen Hybrid Tea. Robinson, 1951. Lydia ×
McGredy's Sunset. It is always difficult to tell why some
roses of great merit still do not become widely planted.
Doreen has never received the acclaim it deserves, for it
is a first-rate, low-growing bedding rose, which will
flower right through the season and seems not to mind
damp and cold. The flowers are large and of a beautiful
shape with the high, pointed centers of the classic bloom,
and many are of exhibition standard. They are a deep
golden orange, with scarlet flushes, growing on a
spreading, bushy plant with dark green, glossy leaves.
It is remarkably healthy for a rose in this color range.

77 Summer Rainbow Hybrid Tea. Jelly, 1966. Peace ×
Dawn. Large, double, high-centered blooms which are
slightly fragrant. They are pink, with the reverse of the
petals yellow, and make a striking bed. Free blooms
grow on a strong, bushy plant which has dark green,
glossy foliage. The rose is not too well known and has
still to make a name for itself.

78 Piccadilly Hybrid Tea. McGredy, 1959. McGredy's
Yellow × Karl Herbst. This is just about the best rose to
have come from that well-known Irish breeder, McGredy.
One parent was the best yellow rose of its time, and the
other, Karl Herbst, was used so often as a parent in
breeding roses that it became known in the rose world as
'The Bull'. Piccadilly is a vigorous, upright grower to
2 ft 6 ins, with very handsome, healthy foliage, changing
from bronze when young to a good, glossy dark green.
The large, high-centered flowers are bright red, with an
equally bright yellow reverse to the petals. As the blooms
age, however, the colors gradually merge and the whole
bloom becomes suffused with a marvellous mixture of red,
gold and orange tones. A showy rose, and certainly the
best bi-color amongst the red and yellow combinations.
It can get both mildew and black spot, but rarely badly.
Only very slight fragrance, but almost always in bloom,
weather-proof, and particularly good in the fall.

78

79 Westminster Hybrid Tea. Robinson, 1960. Gay Crusader × Peace. This rose won a Gold Medal, but it has a good many weaknesses. The large, double blooms are attractive when newly opened and are cherry-red with a yellow reverse, but they soon lose their shape and the colors fade. And, surprisingly for a rose with comparatively few petals, it does not open particularly well in wet weather, and is a poor performer in the fall. It is a tall and lanky grower with not many leaves lower down. The foliage is semi-glossy and mid-green, with bronze tints. On the other hand, it is extremely fragrant.

80 Stella Hybrid Tea, or Grandiflora. Tantau, 1958. Horstmann's Jubiläumsrose × Peace. However you like to classify it, this is one of the loveliest roses ever raised. It has huge, 5 in, high-centered blooms, creamy-white in the center flushed pink and deepening to carmine at the petal edges, with the carmine becoming blush pink in the late season's flowers. A winner at many shows. The flowers repeat quickly, although they tend to come in clusters and to be rather smaller in the fall; this can be stopped by disbudding. They are completely rain-proof, but only slightly scented. An extremely strong and upright grower, which will reach 3 ft, its healthy, dark, glossy leaves sometimes have a bronze tint. One of the small band of roses that is equally good for the garden and for exhibition.

81 Eden Rose Hybrid Tea. Meilland, 1950. Peace × Signora. One of the descendants of Peace which has inherited a lot of its parent's robustness, for it has strong, tall, branching growth, though unlike Peace, it will want watching for mildew. The flowers have a lot of petals and tend to be globular in form and to open quickly, though at their best they have a good shape and have been successful in shows. They have a strong fragrance and are deep pink with a silvery reverse. Glossy, dark green leaves with bronze tints. Not one of the newer roses, but still worth a place in the garden.

82

83

82 Lavendula Floribunda. Kordes, 1965. Magenta ×
Sterling Silver. A reasonably good, lavender-colored
Floribunda, very free with its bloom but rather suspect from
the health point of view. Free, but not very robust growth,
made up for to some extent by its very large and fragrant
flowers, which grow in medium-sized trusses. As with most
roses in this color they tend to fade in strong sunlight. Dark
green leaves. Watch for mildew.

83 Mojave Hybrid Tea. Swim, 1954. Charlotte Armstrong
× Signora. The name is pronounced *Mo-hah-vay* and the rose
was named after the Mojave Indians of North America.
It is a fine rose, even though it does have rather few petals
and in consequence opens quickly. It makes a very striking
display, for its colors are those of a sunset; burnt orange
and flame, prominently veined, with scented and medium
sized blooms. The plant is very tall-growing and erect, so
it is best in small groups at the back of a border, or for
bedding on its own in a fairly large bed. Very healthy and
particularly good late in the year, it has glossy, bronze-green
leaves.

84 Firebeam Floribunda. Fryer, 1960. Masquerade ×
Unknown seedling. 2½ in, semi-double, very strongly scented
flowers carried on good-sized trusses. Vigorous growth and
free bloom. The flowers are a rich blend of flame, yellow and
red, the color holding well as the flower ages. Good, glossy
foliage; some black spot possible.

85 Anna Louisa Floribunda. De Ruiter, 1967. Highlight
× Valeta. Borne in medium-sized to large clusters, the soft
pink flowers are very full and quite delightful. A strong but
low-growing plant that bushes out well, it carries mat,
mid-green leaves which are usually healthy but may get
black spot. It does not mind rain at all. Quite a new
Floribunda, which should have a future if it fulfils its
present promise.

86 Geisha Girl Floribunda. McGredy, 1964. Gold Cup ×
McGredy's Yellow. One of the Floribundas that starts life as
a strong yellow, but fades to cream as the blooms age. The
flowers grow on well-spaced trusses, are about 3½ ins in
diameter, well-shaped at first, but open more or less flat and
rather formless. Tall, branching growth and large, medium-
green, mat leaves which are plentiful, unusually long and
pointed in shape. Very free with its flowers, and a good
repeat.

87 Colour Wonder (Königin der Rosen).   Hybrid Tea.
Kordes, 1964. Parentage unknown. This is a short (2 ft),
compact grower with very thorny stems and shiny, olive-
green leaves. The flowers are very full, with good high
centers, fragrant and of a light nasturtium orange with a
yellow reverse to the petals. It is a most attractive combination
of colors, but unfortunately this rose is not very generous in
its blooming. If cut, the flowers last at least a week in water,
holding their shape perfectly.

88 Margot Fonteyn Hybrid Tea. McGredy, 1964.
Independence × Ma Perkins. 4 in double flowers of 40
petals, of a good shape and coming very freely on a
strong-growing bush. They are very fragrant and colored
rich salmon-orange. Good, mid-green leaves, generally very
healthy.

89 Rose Gaujard Hybrid Tea. Gaujard, 1959. Peace ×
Opera seedling. A good beginner's rose as it is extremely
healthy and robust, and will grow almost anywhere with the
minimum of attention. It produces an abundance of bloom in
all weather, the flowers being of exhibition shape and
quality when at their best, though there is a tendency for
them to come with split centers which does not matter too
much for garden display. They last a long time when cut, and
are pale pink to white, flushed and edged carmine, and with a
silvery reverse. Some fragrance, but it is not strong. The
growth, however, is strong and upright, but branching out
well, with good, glossy, dark green leaves.

86

87

88

89

90

91

90 Zambra Floribunda. Meilland, 1961. (Goldilocks × Fashion) × (Goldilocks × Fashion). This rose when it first comes out is one of the most attractive. Its blooms open flat, are semi-double, and are of the most lovely soft, coppery orange with a bright yellow reverse to the petals. Indeed it is the only rose in this particular color combination, but unfortunately the blooms do not age very well and the petals do not fall cleanly. Instead they turn to a rather dirty pink and need shaking off the plant if the following display is not to be spoiled. As each flush lasts over a long period, and the flowers on the medium-sized trusses open in succession, it is very necessary to do this. The bush is low-growing to about 2 ft or a little more, and spreads out to 3 ft or so. It does, however, follow the pattern of orange roses in that its health is suspect, and black spot is a certainty unless the plant is sprayed. There can be some mildew, too, all of which is a great pity in a rose of unique color. Slight fragrance only.

91 Wisbech Gold Hybrid Tea. McGredy, 1964. Piccadilly × Golden Sun. It is one of the curiosities of rose-breeding that two roses as tall as Piccadilly and Golden Sun should produce the very short Wisbech Gold, which may not exceed 2 ft. But it is a fact that, so mixed is their ancestry, if you cross two roses together you never know for certain what you are going to get. This cross produced an unexpected bonus, because short-growing roses are very much in demand and there are not all that many of them. Despite its low stature, Wisbech Gold is a vigorous and compact grower with good, dark green, glossy leaves. The flowers are large, opening cupped, but are only slightly scented. Golden yellow in color, the petal edges are tinted cerise-pink. A profuse bloomer, but may need protection from mildew.

92 Masquerade Floribunda. Boerner, 1949. Goldilocks × Holiday. This rose really caught the attention of rose growers when it was first introduced 25 years ago. People had forgotten that it was quite usual for roses in Victorian times to change through several colors as they aged, and this is just what Masquerade does. None of the old ones were, however, in its particular color combination. The medium-sized, semi-double flowers, carried on very large trusses, are bright yellow when they first open, turn to salmon-pink and then to a dark and not too attractive red. As the flowers open in succession, all these colors are present in the truss at one time, and it is this gay and very colorful effect that gave the rose its name. There is only slight scent. The bush is strong-growing and will generally reach 3 ft, branching out well.

94

95

96

93 Brasilia Hybrid Tea. McGredy, 1968. Perfecta × Piccadilly. Large, well-shaped blooms, bright scarlet with the reverse silvery white, tinted yellow. They can be as much as 4 ins across. A strong, upright grower with a fair show of flowers. Semi-glossy, medium green leaves; generally very healthy.

94 Princess Margaret of England Hybrid Tea. Meilland, 1968. Queen Elizabeth × (Peace × Michèle Meilland). Not to be confused with Princess Margaret Rose, which is also a pink Hybrid Tea and still in commerce, though not very widely distributed. The latter has small, beautifully shaped flowers on a small bush. Both plant and blooms of Princess Margaret of England are bigger, the flowers being moderately full and of a much stronger phlox pink. They have only a slight scent. Growth is robust, upright, and quite well branched. The leaves are a mat, leathery, light green.

95 Black Velvet Hybrid Tea. Morey, 1960. New Yorker × Happiness. Huge, 5 to 5½ in double flowers with high centers, very well scented and of a deep wine red. As often as not they come singly on good strong stems, which makes them good for cutting. Strong growth, free bloom, and leathery dark leaves. Watch out for mildew.

96 Pernille Poulsen Floribunda. Poulsen, 1965. Ma Perkins × Columbine. In many ways this resembles a low-growing and more compact Elizabeth of Glamis, though the salmon-pink has more pink in it and less salmon, and it does fade much lighter. Although fragrant, it has not the wonderful scent of the latter rose. The flowers are large, often 4 ins across, come very freely on small to medium trusses, and are amongst the first to appear in early summer. The branching bush is well covered in medium-green, semi-glossy leaves, which are unusually long and tapering. Mildew, again, is a possible hazard.

97 Golden Showers Climber. Lammerts, 1956. Charlotte Armstrong × Capt. Thomas. Yet another offspring of Charlotte Armstrong, which has been the seed parent of so many good American roses. This time it produced a rose that is more than just good, for it is one of the few climbers that can truly be called perpetual-flowering. Starting early in the season its long, pointed buds, showing orange at first, open into large, semi-double, fragrant and rather loosely-formed flowers of a quite unfading daffodil yellow. They go on and on blooming on long straight stems, often singly, so that they are good for cutting and last well in water. Not one of the tallest climbers; it will certainly reach 7 or 8 ft, though in the right spot it will go higher, its healthy and glossy dark green leaves clothing a wall or pillar well and showing off the flowers to perfection. It can also be successfully grown, too, as a large free shrub, needing only the minimum of support.

98 Border Coral Floribunda. De Ruiter, 1958. Signal Red × Fashion. A strong, spreading rose of first-rate constitution that bears large trusses of 2½ to 3 in flowers of coral-salmon, yellow tinted at the base of the petals and fragrant. It is very free-flowering and has a good repeat performance. Large, glossy, mid-green leaves. Probably not much above 2 ft in height. As an offspring of two roses not noted for their resistance to disease, it is surprisingly healthy.

99 Sympathie Climber. Kordes, 1964. Parentage unknown. This German rose is one of a very hardy race of climbers and robust shrubs that has been bred for toughness, standing up well to the harsh winters often encountered in northern Europe. Many of them can be grown either as short climbers, suitable for a pillar or low wall, or as large, loose-growing shrubs, so that it is not uncommon to find them under either heading in nursery catalogues. Sympathie is one of the taller ones and will reach 12 ft. It would make a very big shrub indeed and would hardly be suitable for a small garden in this form. The flowers are very full, fragrant, bright red and with a velvety texture to the petals. Glossy, mid-green leaves.

100 Etude Climber. Gregory, 1968. Danse du Feu (Spectacular) × The New Dawn. Flowering in clusters all along its vigorous lateral growths, Etude has good recurrent bloom and is a wall or pillar rose. The medium-sized, semi-double flowers are of a deep salmon-pink and only slightly scented. Very free, branching growth and rather small dark green glossy leaves.

101 Autumn Sunlight Climber. Gregory, 1965. Danse du Feu (Spectacular) × Cl. Goldilocks. Fragrant, rather globular flowers of a bright orange-vermilion. They are of medium size and double, with about 30 petals, and grow in clusters with great abandon. Very vigorous growth and glossy, bright green leaves.

102 Elegance Climber. Brownell, 1937. Glenn Dale × Mary Wallace seedling. It seems right to include one of the older climbers which has stood the test of time, particularly as Elegance has some of the loveliest flowers of any of this group; very large, high-centered, of classic Hybrid Tea form and exhibition standard. Many come singly on long stems, though later in the season they may be in small clusters of three or four and are likely to be rather smaller. They are a soft yellow, deepening towards the heart of the flower, but lack a strong scent, which would have made them perfect. This is not a perpetual-flowering rose, but starts to bloom early in June and will carry on well into July. It may possibly bear a few flowers later, but this is a rare occurrence and cannot be counted on. An enormously strong grower, it will reach 10 to 15 ft, with good light green foliage which may need watching for mildew on dry soils.

100

101   102

103 Pink Perpétue Climber. Gregory, 1965. Danse du Feu (Spectacular) × The New Dawn. This rose has exactly the same parents as Etude, but there are quite a number of differences in the two roses. This one has blooms of clear pink with a carmine pink reverse, which grow in medium-sized clusters. It makes an excellent and very recurrent pillar rose, but though vigorous it does not grow very tall. Only slightly fragrant and with glossy, dark green, rather small leaves.

104 Albertine Barbier, 1921. *Rosa wichuraiana* × Mrs. Arthur Robert Waddell. This is a rose that is usually classified as a rambler, but occasionally you will see it called a climber. Really it seems to be half-way between the two. The flowers are on the large side for a rambler, and they grow just as freely on the old wood of the previous years as they do on the new canes, unlike most ramblers. In June, but not later on, it is literally smothered with its high-centered, medium-sized, coppery-pink blooms, whose scent can be detected from quite a distance. Eventually the flowers open rather loosely and the colour fades a little, but for sheer profusion there is not a rose to beat it. It is enormously vigorous, with rather stiff and thorny growth, and for this reason it is a little surprising that it is sold so often as a weeping standard or tree rose. The whole point of these latter varieties is that the canes should be very pliable and hang down to form a natural umbrella, trailing almost to the ground, as a rambler like Excelsa will do. Albertine will shoot off in all directions and takes considerable training if it is to achieve this effect, though mind you, the struggle is worth it in the end. It can, however, make a spectacular large shrub if you have plenty of space, but will probably need some support. The example in the picture is grown in this way. The semi-glossy, dark green leaves are tinted red when young and are not proof against mildew, though, unlike many of the old ramblers, it can quite easily be controlled by spraying.

106

107

105 Dortmund Kordes, 1955. Seedling × *Rosa kordesii*. Another of the hardy German Kordes roses which were mentioned when describing Sympathie (**99**). This one has very different flowers, single, large, and red with a very distinct white eye. They are very striking and are recurrent, growing in large clusters on a branching but only moderately vigorous plant, which will reach 8 ft as a pillar rose or else make a large specimen bush. The flowers are scented and the leaves dark and glossy.

106 Voie Lactée Climbing Hybrid Tea. Robichon, 1949. Frau Karl Druschki × Luien Pontin. Not very often seen outside its native France, but worth growing if you can obtain it. Coming from globular buds, the flowers open into large, double and very fragrant creamy-white blooms on a strong-growing climber with glossy foliage. Some mildew a possibility, probably inherited from one of its parents, Frau Karl Druschki, one of the most famous white roses of all time, but very prone to attack by disease.

107 Bantry Bay Climber. McGredy, 1967. The New Dawn × Korona. One of a new generation of McGredy climbers and an extremely promising one. The flowers are widely spaced in the trusses and are pink with a touch of salmon, deeper in the center of the blooms. They are of medium size and semi-double, with slight fragrance. A very healthy rose, strong-growing, and with good, glossy mid-green leaves.

108

108 Parade Large-flowered Climber. Boerner, 1957. New Dawn Seedling × Cl. World's Fair. A good, vigorous, repeat-flowering climber, which will reach 10 ft in height and which has glossy, dark green foliage, tinted red. There is a long-lasting and very profuse first flush of bloom in June, some intermittent flowering after that, and then a second flush which is good but does not match the first. Suitable for a wall, fence or pergola, but a bit on the tall side for a pillar. The double flowers, which are only slightly fragrant, are a mixture of carmine and crimson. A good shape at first, they open rather loosely, showing golden stamens. They make a fine display.

There are a number of other good climbers that are worth trying, and nowadays there are many that will flower more than once. For many years it was not considered commercially worthwhile to spend much time or trouble in breeding new varieties, as they were bought in comparatively small numbers. Consequently many of those still in the nursery lists have been going a long time, though only the best of the old ones have survived; and most of these only flower once.

In recent times, on both sides of the Atlantic, things have changed, and now there is a growing number of repeat-flowering climbers to choose from and some that are reasonably recurrent. A number of these have already been described, but here are brief details of a few more that are well worth growing.

Aloha has wonderful, very double, deep pink flowers, sweetly fragrant. It is not a very tall grower and can be used equally well as a shrub. It is quite disease-proof. Casino is a Gold Medal winner and has double, scented blooms of a soft yellow; it will grow up to 9 ft or so. Copenhagen, on the other hand, is bright scarlet. It is fragrant and, like Aloha, will make a good large shrub, as it does not grow much above 8 ft and bushes out well.

With Coral Dawn we are back to the pinks, the scented flowers opening cupped. About 10 ft is its maximum height. Crimson Shower is a rambler, and a comparatively modern one, dating from 1951. True ramblers do not repeat, but on this one the flowers last from July to September. It has the typical rambler clusters of small crimson semi-double flowers. With Danse du Feu, or Spectacular, to use its American name, we are back with the climbers. It is double, orange-scarlet, and has bronze-tinted foliage. There is a good repeat, but it should not be planted in hot, dry soils or bad mildew will be likely.

Handel dates from 1965 and has particularly lovely and unusual blooms, creamy white, flushed pink at the petal edges. Only slight fragrance, but strong growth to 10 or 12 ft. High Noon is a yellow with fragrant semi-double blooms, suitable for a pillar. Joseph's Coat is cherry-red and yellow; another pillar rose or shrub, and very eye-catching.

Extremely free with its flowers and recurrent, Parkdirektor Riggers has blood-red semi-double, 3 in blooms and vigorous growth. Rosy Mantle is one of the newest varieties and dates from 1968. It has moderately full, rose-pink flowers, borne in small clusters, and is covered with glossy, dark green foliage. Schoolgirl has an unusual color for a climber, orange-apricot, and has large, very double and fragrant blooms. And finally, for those who like single roses, there is the crimson-scarlet Soldier Boy; the hips should be removed after the first flowering if a good repeat crop is wanted.